# *Gourmet*
# *Soups*

# *Gourmet Soups*

### Over 75 original recipes
### for adventurous and
### exotic soups

CAROLE CLEMENTS

APPLE

A QUARTO BOOK

Published by The Apple Press
The Old Brewery, 6 Blundell Street
London  N7 9BH

ISBN 1-85076-637-1

This book was designed and produced by
Quarto Publishing Plc
The Old Brewery
6 Blundell Street
London N7 9BH

Art Director: Moira Clinch
Design: Design Revolution
Senior Art Editor: Liz Brown
Copy Editor: Alison Leach
Home Economist: Lucy Miller
Picture Researcher: Susannah Jayes
Picture Manager: Giulia Hetherington
Senior Editor: Sian Parkhouse
Editorial Director: Mark Dartford
Photographer: David Sherwin
Illustrator: Carol Hill

Typeset in Great Britain by
Central Southern Typesetters, Eastbourne
Manufactured in Malaysia by C. H. Colour Scan Sdn. Bhd.
Printed in China by Leefung-Asco Printers Ltd

# Contents

# Introduction:
# *In* PRAISE *of* SOUP

*Every country in the world has its own soup traditions, but it is a universal food. The soup kettle is the great culinary melting pot and the soups in this book come from, or have been inspired by, the traditions of many nations. Some of them combine influences from more than one culture. Learning about the differences and similarities in soup-making around the world has fired my imagination and will, I hope, inspire you equally.*

In some measure, the appeal of soup may well stem from its historical importance – undoubtedly it was one of the earliest forms of cooked food when early man harnessed fire. Through the centuries, people needing sustenance, with little else to fill their bowls, put in pieces of bread and ladled over hot liquid. But soup as we know it is much more than that.

Soup is sometimes served as a hearty breakfast, as is the custom in Périgord and in the eastern Mediterranean. Likewise, it can provide a healthy and satisfying "liquid" lunch. Historically, the evening meal was soup – *souper*, or supper as we now call it, means "to take soup". Soup is a perfect multi-purpose food. You can dress it up or down, eat it for comfort or to excite the palate. The most versatile dish of our diet, it is welcome in all seasons, popular with all generations. It is great for single people – make a big pot and sip it through the week. And you can readily stretch soup to serve an unexpected crowd. You can also give a new life to leftovers, which provide a traditional springboard to delicious soup-making.

A spirit of improvisation is an asset in making soup. Experiment with what is abundantly available and in season – soup is a good way to make the most of a glut of courgettes from the garden or a whole tray of tomatoes reduced for quick sale at the greengrocer. With a dash of common sense and a pinch of caution, soup can be made from almost anything. Skill and confidence come with practice. Look on these

*Endlessly versatile, soup can be prepared from almost anything. This creative aspect makes it as satisfying for the cook as the recipients. Depending on the style, soup may be a light introduction to a meal or a nourishing main course, served up with crusty bread.*

recipes as a framework of basic proportions within which you can modify the ingredients to suit your taste and use your own creativity. Some of the most inspired soups have undoubtedly been the result of experimentation.

The recipes in this book all have a little twist – unusual combinations, a novel ingredient, a certain flair in the presentation, an exotic origin, an interesting history. At the same time, these recipes, many of which are essentially quite simple, rely on three basic principles: a preference for fresh ingredients, careful preparation, thoughtful seasoning. All the soups that require stock will taste better if it is homemade. As stock-making requires time but minimal effort, with a little planning it is easy to have available when you want it.

Many soups can be made in advance and may even improve, with reheating, after the flavours have had time to meld. Reheat soup slowly over a moderate heat just until the ingredients are heated through. If some ingredients, such as seafood, are susceptible to overcooking, strain the soup and return them to the pan of reheated soup just before serving. A microwave is useful for reheating, especially for starchy soups that can easily stick.

Serve chilled soup ice cold and hot soup steaming hot. This may seem elementary, but soup can lose its appeal if it is served lukewarm. A tureen will help soup retain its heat and soup can often be kept warm in its container in a slow oven until you are ready to serve it. Warmed or chilled bowls or serving dishes are essential.

Soup can have a place in any part of the meal. A dramatic soup makes an impressive beginning, but it must be light if the main course is substantial, and if the soup is creamy, this precludes another course with cream. Many soups are perfect as a main course, either following a filling starter or as a satisfying one-course meal with the traditional partner, bread. And why not have soup for dessert? Fruit soups can be a light and novel finish to a memorable meal. There are no rigid rules. Use your imagination and go by what you enjoy.

The selection of wine with soup, or anything else, is so much a matter of personal choice that suggestions must be regarded as no more than signposts pointing in a certain direction. The selections in this book represent what I have enjoyed with a particular soup, but ultimately, your palate is the final adjudicator and you must drink what you like. Some people even believe that serving another liquid with soup is inappropriate; others, however, believe that no course is complete without wine. Again, you must follow your own inclinations. Experiment with what you think you might like and what you have available.

Making soup is a creative endeavour. It is rewarding for both the cook and the recipients. The wisps of steam wafting from a soup pot simmering on the stove permeate the atmosphere not just with an aroma, but also with an evocation of hearth, home and history.

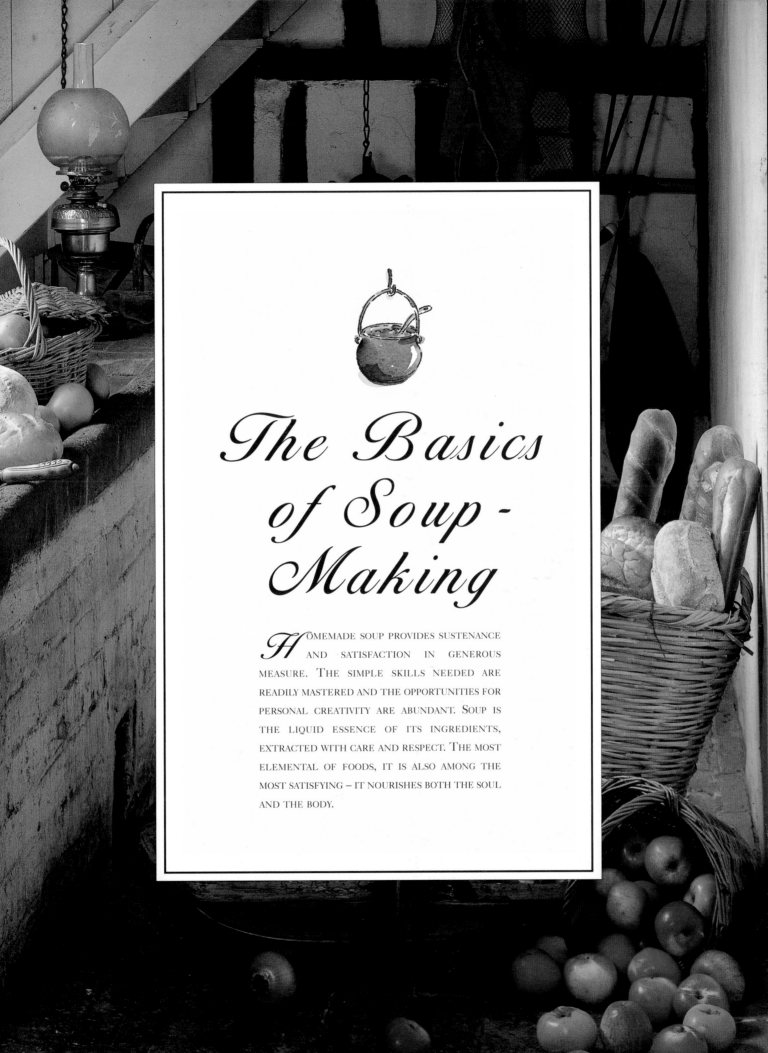

# The Basics of Soup - Making

HOMEMADE SOUP PROVIDES SUSTENANCE AND SATISFACTION IN GENEROUS MEASURE. THE SIMPLE SKILLS NEEDED ARE READILY MASTERED AND THE OPPORTUNITIES FOR PERSONAL CREATIVITY ARE ABUNDANT. SOUP IS THE LIQUID ESSENCE OF ITS INGREDIENTS, EXTRACTED WITH CARE AND RESPECT. THE MOST ELEMENTAL OF FOODS, IT IS ALSO AMONG THE MOST SATISFYING – IT NOURISHES BOTH THE SOUL AND THE BODY.

# *The* BASICS *of* SOUP-MAKING

*S*oup is one of the easiest things to make and homemade soup is worth the small effort it takes. It is as economical as it is appealing, needing no fancy equipment or extravagant ingredients for good results.

## *Equipment*

Soup-making requires very little in the way of equipment, but you will need a large saucepan – a 3l/5pt capacity pan with a lid is really the minimum – or a large, deep enamelled iron casserole. If you make stock often, a tall, narrow stockpot with handles (it is quite heavy when filled) is a worthwhile investment. Stainless steel or another nonreactive material such as enamel is advisable to avoid discoloration with acidic and other ingredients that react negatively with certain metals; aluminium is best avoided for this reason. For easy cleaning, stainless steel is excellent.

Sharp knives are essential. You should have at least a paring knife and a long wide-bladed chef's knife, as well as a good-sized chopping board or two, preferably non-porous and dishwasher-proof, and a swivel-bladed vegetable peeler. Kitchen scissors and a cleaver are also useful, as well as various long-handled spoons and kitchen string. All of these you are likely to have in your kitchen already, but you may not have acquired a skimmer, a flat round utensil, perforated or with a wire-mesh insert, used to lift off the scum or froth from stock. For this, a large perforated spoon will also do, but a skimmer makes it easier. For stock-making and for many soups, you will need a sieve and colander. It helps to have several sizes and types: a large fine-mesh wire sieve, a nylon mesh sieve for foods that discolour, a colander for draining, and perhaps a conical sieve and a drum sieve, if space and budget permit.

When working with large quantities, a large 2l/3½pt measuring container is more useful than the usual small size. I also find a large capacity fat separator, also known as a degreasing jug, invaluable when you need to use freshly made stock and there is no time to chill it and allow the fat to congeal for removal. This is simply a jug with the spout at the bottom so you can pour the grease-free liquid from the bottom and stop pouring when the fat on top reaches the level of the spout.

When a soup is puréed, the smoothness of the result depends on the equipment used: a food mill, food processor, blender or immersible electric hand blender will each process the food in a slightly different way. A food mill is handy because it purées and sieves at the same time. It consists of a rotary blade which is turned with a hand crank against a perforated disc, available with perforations of various sizes allowing more or less of the solid matter to pass through. The apparatus is set over a saucepan or bowl, with legs and a handle to steady it. This simple, inexpensive utensil is found in almost every European kitchen and its merits are being rediscovered elsewhere.

The food processor is probably the most widely available electrical appliance today. It produces a purée that is smooth but not homogenous and if there are seeds or fibres, the purée will need to be sieved. The most successful technique is to purée the solids with just a little of the liquid, then thin the purée with the remainder of the liquid afterwards, rather than to process several watery batches.

A blender produces the smoothest results. Because the strong suction that draws food to the blades creates a whirlpool effect, the food is homogenized in a way that the food mill or processor is incapable of producing. This is particularly advantageous in many puréed vegetable soups where a silky texture is desirable and even soups made of relatively fibrous vegetables, such as pumpkin, do not need sieving after being puréed in a blender. An electric hand blender, a tall wand with small crossed blades like a blender, produces similar results in many instances, and since it is immersed in the cooking pan, cleaning up is easier.

There are advantages and also some drawbacks to each of these appliances. If you are making a large quantity of soup, the relatively limited capacity of a food processor or blender means that puréeing will have to be done in batches, unless you have a professional-sized model. Do not fill the containers more than about halfway. With a processor, liquid may leak around the top and under the blade assembly. With a blender, the suction action creates a cyclone that can push against the lid and lift it even when you are holding it down. It is advisable with either one to allow soup ingredients to cool somewhat before puréeing and to protect yourself from escaping liquid with a towel or oven glove.

## Ingredients

Many delicious soups are made with water. It is economical and readily available, and it allows the taste of other ingredients to come through. Although stock can be an important element, there is no need to use stock if a soup has plenty of flavour without it.

Stock is essentially flavoured water. It is the cooking liquid of meat, poultry, game or fish and/or their bones simmered with vegetables, herbs and water or some combination of these. Meat, poultry and fish stock add body as well as flavour to soups or other preparations because of the gelatine derived from the bones. A stock made of vegetables and herbs will provide flavour, but not body.

Soup can only be as good as the ingredients from which it is made. Soups and stocks often provide an opportunity to use food that is just past its prime and to give new life to leftovers, but the fresher the ingredients, the more they have to impart, both in terms of flavour and nutrients.

The soup recipes in this book assume peeling of those vegetables which are normally peeled for cooking, such as garlic and onions, and soaking or rinsing of those vegetables that tend to be gritty, such as leeks and spinach. Carrots may be peeled or not, according to condition and personal preference, and potatoes used in soups are generally peeled except for small ones. For stock-making, peeling is not usually essential, apart from vegetables which have been waxed, but all vegetables should be thoroughly scrubbed with a brush under running water. When the zest of citrus fruits is used, unwaxed fruit is preferable; otherwise wash in warm soapy water and rinse well.

Herbs used to flavour soups and stocks are often tied tightly in a bundle to facilitate removal after cooking. This herb bundle, called a bouquet garni, usually contains 4–6 parsley stems or sprigs, 3–4 fresh thyme sprigs, 1–2 bay leaves and sometimes a piece of leek or small leafy celery stick, but it might also contain herbs appropriate to a particular dish, such as sage, tarragon or dill. When preparing a large quantity of soup, make a bigger bouquet garni, increasing the ingredients and wrapping them in leek greens or bay leaves before securing with kitchen string.

*Soup-making requires only simple equipment, most of which will already be at hand in your kitchen. Remember that the best ingredients make the best soups and those made from good quality raw materials, carefully selected and prepared, will have the most flavour.*

# Stock-Making

*S*tock, the foundation of many soups, is almost effortless to make. It needs more patience than skill and yields a delectable liquid ready to consume as a clear soup or to use as the basis for other soups, transformed with an array of additions.

The French word for stock, *fond,* also means base, foundation – and stock provides the foundation for many soups, as well as some sauces and stews. Stock is easy to make as it requires almost no attention after the initial stages and

*A variety of vegetables and even fruit can be used for stock-making. Adjust the ingredients according to what you have available, but use strongly flavoured vegetables sparingly. A stock made without bones needs plenty of vegetables and herbs for good flavour.*

virtually cooks itself. Ready-prepared stocks are widely available now and many are tasty, but they tend to be expensive. Homemade stock is easy and economical. The ingredients for stock can vary enormously, and should reflect what you have available, with some consideration given to the eventual purpose of the stock. In addition to the bones of meat or poultry or fish, aromatic vegetables, such as carrot, onion and garlic, are essential. Other vegetables, including leeks or their greens, shallots, mushrooms, parsnips, celery or celeriac, may also be in-

cluded. Keep in mind that strongly flavoured vegetables like cabbage, kale or swede should be used with discretion and avoided in stocks destined for delicate soups.

Vegetarian stocks need more than just the usual aromatic vegetables to give them depth of flavour. Lettuce, cabbage, spinach or other greens, additional herbs and a substantial amount of the above vegetables should be used. Include some sweet ones, such as parsnips or celeriac, or a small apple or pear.

Unless you buy your meat at a butcher or a supermarket where meat is cut on the premises, it is not always easy to obtain meat bones for stock. Veal bones give more flavour than beef bones. Chicken bones are more readily available, and a rich brown chicken stock can be used in place of meat stock in most recipes.

It is best not to add salt to stock; it will be concentrated during evaporation or reduction. Season your soup, or whatever you are making, after adding stock.

## Procedure

Use cold water in stock-making; it helps to extract impurities and enables the ingredients to yield their flavour. Remember that the water should be in proportion to the rest of the ingredients – in other words, don't drown them. The amount varies with the container used and the density of the ingredients in it, but for maximum flavour, keep the stock ingredients covered with about 2.5cm/1in of water, and top up with cold water if the level of the liquid falls below the solids.

When a richer flavour or deeper colour is needed, brown the ingredients by roasting or sautéeing them before adding to the stockpot.

Skimming is vital. The scum or foam is impurities rising to the surface; if not removed, they will cook into the stock and it will be cloudy. Well skimmed, slowly "brewed" stock can be remarkably clear.

Cook stock uncovered, or partially covered, and avoid boiling it. Boiling clouds stock and causes fat to be emulsified or incorporated into the liquid; it is not then possible to remove it or its greasy taste. If the pot is covered, the stock is likely to boil no matter how low the heat under it, and it may sour. Meat stock needs 4–6 hours of simmering to extract all the goodness from the ingredients, but poultry stock only requires about half this time, up to 3 hours. Simmer fish stock for about 30 minutes; if cooked too long, it can acquire a bitter taste.

Strain stock through a fine-meshed sieve as soon as it is ready. For the most limpid stock, line the sieve with damp muslin.

Remove the fat before using stock. Either chill to allow the fat to congeal on top and lift it off, or pour warm stock into a fat separator, or degreasing jug, let it stand until the fat rises to the top, then pour off the lean stock through the spout at the bottom. You can also spoon off the fat, but this is less effective.

If the taste of your stock is insipid, reduce it to concentrate the flavour. Soups in which stock is the major element must be rich in flavour. Reduction is also used to concentrate the volume for storage. If you want completely clear stock, as for consommé, it must always be clarified. Since the clarification process removes some of the stock's original flavour, other ingredients are added to fortify it, cut into small pieces to yield flavour quickly, but the clarification itself is actually accomplished by the addition of egg whites, usually 1 white per 1l/1¾pt.

Fresh stock keeps for about 3 days, refrigerated, and it can be boiled again and stored for a further 2–3 days. It can be reduced to a glaze and refrigerated or frozen in ice-cube trays; the cubes can then be added to soups and sauces to enrich texture and flavour without defrosting.

*The shape of a stockpot permits the slow reduction of liquid, so it is as good for a long simmered meat stock as a quickly made seafood stock. Because the vegetables and other ingredients are densely packed, the proportion of water is usually right.*

~.~.~.~.~.~.~.~.~.~

## *Stock-Making Tips*

*Save stock ingredients in the freezer as you accumulate them: poultry giblets, necks, backs and carcasses, scraps and cooked bones from roasts, trimmings and raw bones from poultry or meat you have boned yourself, clean vegetable trimmings such as leek greens, spring onion tops, mushroom stalks, celery leaves and pithy branches, slightly wilted herbs or the remaining half onions when you have chopped the other half.*
*Store in tightly sealed plastic freezer bags or boxes. Although the flavour never equals that of homemade, sometimes it may be necessary to rely on stock made from stock cubes or granules. For a more balanced flavour, add half again or twice the amount of water indicated in the instructions and simmer for about 30 minutes with aromatic vegetables and herbs. Canned beef consommé is useful to have to hand, but it also benefits from diluting with water and simmering with herbs if time permits.*

~.~.~.~.~.~.~.~.~.~

# Stock Recipes

*U*se the following stock recipes as a framework for stock-making. Make smaller or larger batches or vary the ingredients, if you wish, but be sure to use enough ingredients in your stock to give give good flavour or it will need to be reduced to concentrate the flavour and some of the volume will be lost.

## MEAT STOCK

A variety of ingredients may be used in making meat stock. Veal bones give more flavour than beef bones, but they are not easy to obtain. If the bones have no meat on them, it is best to add some stewing beef. You can also use a meaty cut like shin, preferably on the bone, with a few pieces of oxtail and/or chicken necks, backs or carcasses to provide gelatine. Avoid lamb bones unless you want to make lamb stock.

**MAKES ABOUT 2.5L/4½PT**

*2.5–3kg • 6–7lb meaty bones and meat (including veal or beef knuckle, shin or other bones, oxtails, bones from roasts, poultry carcasses and/or poultry necks, giblets, etc)*
*2 large unpeeled onions, halved and root end trimmed*
*2 carrots, scrubbed and cut in large pieces*
*1 celery stick, cut in large pieces*
*2 leeks, cut in large pieces*
*1–2 parsnips, cut in large pieces (optional)*
*2–4 unpeeled garlic cloves, lightly crushed*
*large bouquet garni (parsley stems, thyme sprigs, celery leaves and bay leaf)*
*3–4 cloves (optional)*
*6–8 allspice berries (optional)*

❶ Put the bones and meat, the onions, carrots, celery, leeks, parsnips, if using, and garlic in a large stockpot or heavy saucepan, pushing the vegetables down between the bones. Cover with cold water by at least 5cm/2in and bring to the boil over medium-high heat. As the liquid heats, foam will begin to appear on the surface. As soon as it appears and until it stops surfacing, skim off the foam with a skimmer or perforated spoon.
❷ When the stock reaches boiling point, reduce the heat to low and add the bouquet garni and spices, if using. Simmer very slowly, uncovered, for about 4–5 hours, skimming occasionally and topping up with cold water if the liquid level falls below the solids. Gently ladle the stock through a sieve, lined with damp muslin if you wish, into a large container.
❸ To remove the fat, chill the stock to allow it to congeal, then scrape off the fat. Gently remove any further traces of fat by wiping a paper towel lightly across the surface. If time is short, use a fat separator to remove the fat from the warm stock or spoon off the fat. Blot any remaining beads of fat with paper towels.
❹ If you wish, reduce the stock to concentrate the flavour. Store in the refrigerator or freezer.

### Ham Stock

See Ham and Split Pea Soup, Page 53

## BROWN STOCK

Put the bones, meat and vegetables in a large roasting tin and brown in a preheated 230°C/450°F/Gas 8 oven for 30–40 minutes, turning occasionally. Transfer the ingredients to the stockpot, discarding the fat, and add the bouquet garni, cloves and allspice berries. Proceed as for Meat Stock.

# CHICKEN STOCK

Chicken bones are more readily available than meat bones, so chicken stock is easier – as well as quicker – to make. If you want cooked chicken meat for your soup, or for another purpose, use a whole boiling fowl or roasting chicken.

**MAKES ABOUT 2L/3½PT**

*2kg • 4½lb raw chicken backs, necks, feet or raw or cooked carcasses or whole or cut up (jointed) chicken*
*2 large unpeeled onions, root end trimmed*
*3 carrots, scrubbed, cut in large pieces*
*1 celery stick, cut in large pieces*
*1 leek, cut in large pieces*
*2 unpeeled garlic cloves, lightly crushed*
*large bouquet garni (parsley stems, thyme and marjoram or tarragon sprigs and bay leaf)*

Proceed as for Meat Stock, but simmer for only 2–3 hours. If using a whole bird or pieces, cut off the breast meat after 25–30 minutes and return the remainder to the stockpot.

## *Variations*

### *Brown Chicken Stock*
Brown the chicken pieces in a frying pan over medium heat until golden and transfer to the stockpot, discarding the fat. Proceed as for Chicken Stock.

### *Turkey Stock*
Remove any stuffing, break or chop the carcass into pieces and, if you wish, add sage leaves to the bouquet garni. Proceed as for Chicken Stock.

### *Game Stock*
Proceed as for Chicken Stock, with or without initial browning.

# FISH STOCK

Fish stock is quick and easy to make. The initial cooking of the fish parts in butter makes a richer stock, but if you wish, omit this step and combine all the ingredients in the stockpot. Avoid using the bones of oily fish, such as mackerel or salmon for all-purpose stock.

**MAKES ABOUT 1.5L/2¾PT**

*15g • ½oz butter*
*900g • 2lb heads, bones and trimmings from fresh white fish*
*1 onion, thinly sliced*
*1 carrot, thinly sliced*
*1 leek, thinly sliced*
*250ml • 8fl oz dry white wine*
*1.2l • 2pt water*
*6–8 parsley stems*
*6–8 black peppercorns*

❶ Melt the butter in a large nonreactive saucepan or flameproof casserole over medium-high heat and add the fish parts. Cook for 2–3 minutes and add the vegetables, wine, water, parsley stems and peppercorns.
❷ Bring to the boil, skimming off any foam that rises to the top. Reduce the heat to low and simmer gently for 25 minutes. Strain through a muslin-lined sieve and remove any fat.

# SHELLFISH STOCK

Don't throw away the shells of crustaceans. Make this stock with the shells of prawns, scampi or lobster you have enjoyed for another meal.

**MAKES ABOUT 1.5L/2¾PT**

*250–450g • 8oz–1lb prawn shells and heads, scampi or lobster shells, heads and legs*
*1 onion, chopped*
*1 small carrot, sliced*
*1 celery stick, sliced*
*½ lemon (unwaxed or scrubbed), thinly sliced*
*1.5l • 2¾pt water*
*bouquet garni (parsley stems, thyme sprigs and leek greens)*

❶ Combine the shellfish shells, heads and parts with the vegetables, lemon and water in a saucepan. Bring to the boil, skimming off any foam that rises to the top.
❷ Reduce the heat to low and simmer gently, partially covered, for 25 minutes. Strain the stock through a muslin-lined sieve and remove any fat.

# VEGETABLE STOCK

With vegetable stock, it is even more important to balance the proportion of water to ingredients and to give some thought to the eventual use of the stock so you can select suitable ingredients. Cut the vegetables more finely than for long-simmered stocks so they can yield their goodness quickly and include plenty of other seasonal vegetables along with the basic ones.

**MAKES ABOUT 2L/3½PT**

*1 large onion, halved and thinly sliced*
*2 shallots, thinly sliced*
*2 carrots, thinly sliced*
*1 parsnip, thinly sliced*
*1 large leek, thinly sliced*
*1–2 turnips or ½ swede, halved and thinly sliced*
*1 potato, cut in large chunks*
*50–75g • 2–3oz mushrooms or mushroom stems*

*50–70g • 2–3oz green beans or green bean trimmings (optional)*
*150–175g • 5–6oz cabbage, or 75–115g • 3–4oz other greens, such as lettuce, chard or kale*
*large bouquet garni (parsley stems, thyme and marjoram sprigs, a few rosemary or sage leaves and 1–2 bay leaves)*

❶ Combine the ingredients in a large stockpot, add cold water to cover by at least 2.5cm/1in and bring to the boil over medium-high heat, skimming off any foam that rises to the top.
❷ Reduce the heat to low and simmer gently for about 45 minutes. Strain the stock through a muslin-lined sieve and remove any fat.

# GARLIC STOCK

This herb and garlic infusion is a basic vegetable stock that you can make quickly with ingredients you are likely to have on hand.

**MAKES ABOUT 1.5L/2¾PT**

*1.5l • 2¾pt water*
*1 large garlic bulb (about 20 garlic cloves), unpeeled*
*4–6 thyme sprigs, or 2.5ml • ½tsp dried thyme*

*6 marjoram sprigs, or 2.5ml • ½tsp dried marjoram*
*bay leaf*

❶ Combine the water, garlic, thyme, marjoram and bay leaf in a saucepan.
❷ Bring to the boil, reduce the heat to medium-low and simmer, partially covered, for 30–45 minutes then strain.

# SPICED VEGETABLE STOCK

This Indian-spiced stock makes a good base for curried soups or stews.

**MAKES ABOUT 1.5L/2¾PT**

*1tbsp vegetable oil*
*1 large onion, sliced*
*1 large leek, sliced*
*2 carrots, chopped*
*1 celery stick with leaves, sliced*
*2 garlic cloves, peeled and crushed*
*5ml • 1tsp coriander seed*
*3 cardamom pods*

*2 cloves*
*½tsp each cumin seed and mustard seed*
*½tsp each dried thyme and oregano*
*1.5l • 2¾pt water*
*6–8 parsley stems*
*½ lemon (unwaxed or scrubbed), thinly sliced*

❶ Heat the oil in a large heavy saucepan or stockpot over medium heat. Add the onion, leek, carrots and celery, and cook until the onion becomes softer and slightly transparent. Add the spices and dried herbs, and continue cooking for 2–3 minutes.
❷ Stir in the water, parsley and lemon, and bring to the boil. Reduce the heat to low and simmer for 30–40 minutes. Strain the stock and remove any fat.

~.~.~.~.~.~.~.~.~.~.~

*COOK'S TIP*
The addition of spices can contribute
to an interesting stock, but they should
only be used when it is destined for a
soup you know they will enhance.
Otherwise wait and add spices
to the soup itself.

~.~.~.~.~.~.~.~.~.~.~

# CHAPTER ONE

# Vegetable Soups

Soup is a perfect way to celebrate the abundant profusion of each vegetable as the growing season progresses – from spring asparagus to full-blown summer vegetables such as tomatoes, peppers and aubergines to autumn's colourful pumpkins to the chestnuts and beans that we welcome in winter. The following recipes offer exciting vegetable soups for every month of the year.

# VEGETABLE SOUPS

*V*egetables provide limitless opportunity for soup-making. Their versatility makes them a logical choice, whether you want a light and refreshing purée of fresh greens, a thick creamy chowder or a robust tomato soup.

Many of these soups feature vegetables puréed to a smooth velvety consistency that puts the focus on their unique flavour. These usually have only one or two main ingredients, so the flavour is distinct. Often no additional thickening is used, as the vegetables themselves provide the needed bulk. A little cream is a pleasant addition, but this is always optional. Puréed soups have a certain formality that makes them perfect served as first courses, but they are equally satisfying at other times.

Compound soups, like Provençal Vegetable Soup or Tuscan Bean and Kale Soup, tend to be heartier but may be less rich. They contain a variety of ingredients which are eaten with their cooking

Almost any vegetable is good made into soup, whether a smooth purée, such as asparagus soup, or a chunky mixture, like vegetable chowder. Some vegetables are an asset to any soup – potato, for instance, is often added to thicken other soups.

*liquid and such soups may be thick or thin, depending on the density of the vegetables in them.*

*Leftovers can be the springboard for vegetable soups, as well as other kinds. Just bring your creativity and common sense to the task and give some thought to how flavours will combine. Start by cooking an onion in butter, with perhaps other aromatic vegetables, such as carrot and leek or garlic – just as most of the soups in this chapter begin. A straightforward recipe, like Sweet Potato and Leek Soup, can provide the basic procedure. Then you can substitute leftovers – for instance, mashed potatoes in place of the sweet and white potatoes in the recipe.*

*These soups can all be adapted to your own taste. A little more tomato, a little less cream, a little different seasoning may well be an improvement.*

~.~.~.~.~.~.~.~.~.~.

*"Beautiful soup, so rich and green,*
*Waiting for a hot tureen,*
*Who for such dainties would not stoop?*
*Soup of the evening, beautiful soup!"*

ALICE IN WONDERLAND
*Lewis Carroll, 1832–98*

~.~.~.~.~.~.~.~.~

# PROVENCAL VEGETABLE SOUP

*(Soupe au Pistou)*

The *pistou*, a kind of Provençal *pesto* sauce which is stirred in at the end, gives this vegetable soup a special zing, so don't leave it out. The assortment of vegetables, however, can be varied according to availability.

**SERVES 6**

275g • 10oz fresh shelled broad, coco or cranberry beans, or 175g • 6oz dried beans, soaked overnight
¼tsp dried herbes de Provence
2 garlic cloves, minced
1tbsp olive oil
1 medium onion, finely chopped
1 large leek, split and finely sliced
1 celery stick, finely sliced
2 thin carrots, finely diced
2 small potatoes, finely diced
115g • 4oz thin French beans
1.2l • 2pt water

salt and freshly ground pepper
115g • 4oz shelled peas, fresh or frozen
2 small courgettes, quartered lengthwise and finely sliced
3 medium tomatoes, peeled, deseeded and finely chopped
a handful of spinach leaves, cut in thin ribbons

BASIL PUREE
1 large or 2 small garlic cloves, very finely chopped
15g • ½oz basil leaves
4tbsp freshly grated Parmesan cheese
4tbsp extra-virgin olive oil

❶ To make the basil purée, put the garlic, basil and cheese in a food processor fitted with a metal blade and process until thoroughly puréed, scraping down the sides once. With the machine running, slowly pour the olive oil through the feed tube. Alternatively, pound the garlic, basil and cheese in a pestle and mortar, then stir in the oil.

❷ Put the fresh or soaked beans in a large saucepan with the herbs and 1 of the garlic cloves, and add water to cover by 2.5cm/1in. Bring to the boil, reduce the heat and simmer over moderately low heat until the beans are cooked, about 30 minutes for fresh beans, or about 1 hour for dried beans. Set aside in the cooking liquid.

❸ Heat the olive oil in a large saucepan over medium-low heat. Add the onion and leek, and cook for 5 minutes, stirring occasionally, until the onion softens. Add the celery, carrots and the remaining garlic, and cook, covered, for another 10 minutes, stirring frequently.

❹ Add the potatoes, French beans and water. Season lightly with salt and pepper. Bring to the boil, reduce the heat to low and simmer, covered, for 10 minutes.

❺ Add the peas, courgettes and tomatoes. Add the cooked broad beans with the cooking liquid and simmer for 25–30 minutes, or until all the vegetables are tender. Taste for seasoning. Add the spinach and simmer for 5 minutes longer. Ladle into warmed bowls and swirl a spoonful of basil purée into each.

# TUSCAN WHITE BEAN *and* KALE SOUP

This soup is perfect for a fireside supper on a winter's evening. Serve it with warm focaccio or garlic bread.

**SERVES 6**

*225g • 8oz dried borlotti beans (or haricot beans), soaked overnight in cold water to cover generously*
*1tbsp olive oil*
*100g • 3½oz pancetta or smoked lean bacon, chopped*
*1 onion, finely chopped*
*1 shallot, finely chopped*
*1 carrot, finely chopped*
*1–2 garlic cloves, minced*
*4 tomatoes, peeled, deseeded and chopped, or*

*400g • 14oz canned chopped tomatoes*
*1.2l • 2pt water*
*bouquet garni (thyme and marjoram sprigs, parsley stems and bay leaf)*
*115g • 4oz curly kale leaves, finely chopped (from 1 small bunch, stems discarded)*
*freshly grated or shaved Parmesan cheese, for serving (optional)*

❶ Drain the beans, put into a saucepan with cold water to cover and set over high heat. Bring to the boil and boil for 10 minutes. Drain and add fresh cold water to cover. Bring to the boil again, drain and rinse well.

❷ Heat the oil in a large heavy saucepan over medium-high heat and add the pancetta or bacon. Cook until lightly browned, stirring frequently. Remove with a slotted spoon to drain on paper towels and pour off all but 1tbsp of the fat. Reduce the heat to low, add the onion, shallot, carrot and garlic, and cook for 3–4 minutes until slightly softened. Add the beans, tomatoes, water, bouquet garni and pancetta or bacon, and simmer until the beans are tender, 1–2 hours. Season to taste with salt and pepper.

❸ Stir in the kale and continue cooking for 15–20 minutes, or until it is tender. Adjust the seasoning and ladle the soup into warmed bowls. Serve sprinkled with Parmesan cheese, if you wish.

~.~.~.~.~.~.~.~.~.~

*TO DRINK*
A medium-dry red wine, such as Côtes de Provence or Navarra.

~.~.~.~.~.~.~.~.~.~

# EMERALD SOUP

In this gloriously coloured soup, the sharpness of the watercress is tamed by the pear. It is pretty served in glass bowls.

**SERVES 4**

*15g • ½oz butter*
*1 large onion, chopped*
*1 small potato, diced*
*1l • 1¾ pt chicken stock*
*bouquet garni (1 sprig each*
*    fresh marjoram and thyme*
*    and 1 bay leaf)*
*1 large ripe pear, cored, peeled*
*    and chopped*

*1 bunch watercress, washed*
*    and stems discarded, about*
*    50g • 2oz leaves*
*450g • 1lb young spinach,*
*    washed and stems discarded*
*salt and freshly ground pepper*
*freshly ground nutmeg*
*watercress sprigs, to garnish*

❶ Melt the butter in a heavy saucepan over medium heat. Add the onion and cook until golden, 3–4 minutes. Add the potato, stock and bouquet garni. Cook gently until the vegetables are tender, about 25 minutes.
❷ Stir in the pear and cook for 2 minutes. Remove the bouquet garni. Add the watercress and spinach, and continue cooking for 3–4 minutes, stirring frequently until the leaves are completely wilted.
❸ Transfer the soup to a blender or a food processor fitted with a steel blade and purée until smooth, working in batches if necessary. Return to the saucepan and season to taste with salt, pepper and nutmeg. Set over medium-low heat and simmer for 4–5 minutes until reheated. Ladle into warmed bowls or soup plates and garnish with watercress sprigs.

# JERUSALEM ARTICHOKE SOUP

This native North American vegetable was introduced in England from Massachusetts. It was a favourite of the Victorians and this silky, genteel soup is typical.

**SERVES 3–4**

*1 lemon (unwaxed or scrubbed)*
*450g • 1lb Jerusalem artichokes*
*15g • ½oz butter*
*1 shallot, chopped*
*½ onion, chopped*
*750ml • 1¼pt white chicken or*
*    veal stock*

*3tbsp whipping cream*
*salt and white pepper*
*borage flowers or flat-leafed*
*    parsley, to garnish*

❶ Finely grate the zest from the lemon and set aside. Fill a bowl with cold water and add the juice of ½ lemon. Reserve the other ½ lemon.
❷ Peel the Jerusalem artichokes and cut large ones in two or three pieces. Drop into the acidulated water to prevent discoloration.
❸ Melt the butter in a heavy saucepan over medium heat. Add the shallot and onion and cook, stirring frequently, until just softened, about 4 minutes. Drain the Jerusalem artichokes and add them to the pan with the stock. Bring just to the boil, reduce the heat to medium-low and simmer gently until the vegetables are tender, 15–20 minutes.
❹ Transfer the solids to a blender or a food processor fitted with a steel blade, add some of the cooking liquid and purée until smooth. Return to the saucepan with the remaining cooking liquid, add the cream, salt, pepper and lemon zest and juice to taste. Set over medium-low heat and simmer for 3–5 minutes until reheated. Ladle the soup into warmed bowls and float a borage flower or parsley leaf on top.

# AUBERGINE *and* RED PEPPER SOUP

Roasting the aubergine before making the soup gives a rich, mellow flavour. If you wish, you can roast the vegetables up to 2 days ahead. Refrigerate them, wrapped, until needed.

**SERVES 4–6**

| | |
|---|---|
| *2 large aubergines* | *1l · 1¾pt chicken stock* |
| *2 large red peppers* | *pinch of dried thyme* |
| *Tabasco sauce* | *5–6 coriander seeds* |
| *2tsp olive oil* | *1tsp concentrated tomato paste* |
| *1 large onion, finely chopped* | *6tbsp whipping cream* |
| *3 garlic cloves, finely chopped* | *salt and pepper* |

❶ Preheat the oven to 200°C/400°F/Gas 6. Place the aubergines and peppers in a shallow roasting tin and roast until the pepper skins are evenly darkened, about 1 hour, turning the vegetables three or four times. Put the peppers in a sturdy plastic bag, seal tightly and leave to steam.

❷ When the vegetables are cool enough to handle, peel the aubergines and cut into cubes. Working over a bowl to catch the liquid, peel the skin from the peppers and remove the cores and seeds. Put the pepper flesh in a food processor fitted with a steel blade and strain in the liquid. Purée until smooth and season with Tabasco. Scrape into a small bowl and set aside.

❸ Heat the oil in a large heavy saucepan over medium-low heat. Add the onion and cook for 4–5 minutes, stirring frequently, until just softened. Add the garlic and continue cooking for 1 minute longer. Add the aubergine cubes, stock, thyme, coriander seeds and tomato paste. Cover and simmer for 30 minutes, or until the vegetables are very tender.

❹ Transfer the solids to a blender or a food processor fitted with a steel blade. Add some of the cooking liquid and purée until smooth, working in batches if necessary. Return the purée to the saucepan with the remaining cooking liquid, stir in the cream and adjust the seasoning, if necessary. Reheat the soup over medium-low heat for about 5 minutes, or until heated through. Ladle into warmed bowls and top each serving with a dollop of the red pepper purée, dividing it evenly.

~.~.~.~.~.~.~.~.~.~

*TO DRINK*
A medium-bodied
fruity red wine, such
as Pinotage or
Beaujolais.

~.~.~.~.~.~.~.~.~.~

# PUMPKIN *and* COCONUT SOUP

Served from a hollowed-out pumpkin, this spicy soup makes a dramatic and tasty starter. It is best to use another pumpkin for serving, as it is difficult to carve the flesh from the inside without piercing the shell. Cut enough from the top to make a wide opening – like a bowl – and scrape out the seeds and filaments. Warm the pumpkin shell in a slow oven or fill with boiling water and empty before filling with soup. Of course, the soup can be ladled into a warmed tureen or individual bowls.

**SERVES 6**

*milk from 1 coconut*
*15g • ½oz butter*
*1 large onion, chopped*
*1 large potato, cubed*
*2 garlic cloves, minced*
*800g • 1¾lb pumpkin, cubed*
*100g • 3½oz grated fresh*
  *coconut*
*4tsp finely chopped fresh*
  *root ginger*

*¼tsp dried chilli flakes*
*grated nutmeg*
*bouquet garni (thyme sprigs,*
  *parsley stems, lemon grass*
  *and bay leaf)*
*175ml • 6fl oz whipping cream*
*6tbsp coconut cream*
*salt and freshly ground pepper*
*toasted coconut strips, to*
  *garnish*

❶ Empty the coconut milk through a fine-mesh sieve lined with damp muslin into a large measuring container. Add water to make 1.2l/2pt.

❷ Melt the butter in a large heavy saucepan over medium-low heat, add the onion and cook until just softened, about 4 minutes.

❸ Add the potato, garlic, pumpkin and the diluted coconut milk to the saucepan. Bring to the boil, then reduce the heat to medium-low. Add the grated coconut, root ginger, red pepper flakes, a generous grating of nutmeg and the bouquet garni. Simmer, stirring occasionally, until the vegetables are very tender, 15–20 minutes.

❹ Remove the bouquet garni and transfer the solids to a blender or a food processor fitted with a steel blade. Add some of the cooking liquid and purée until smooth, working in batches if necessary. Return the purée to the pan with the remaining liquid and stir in the cream. Season to taste with salt and pepper.

❺ Reheat the soup gently over low heat. Pour or ladle the soup into a warm pumpkin shell, or a tureen or bowls, and sprinkle with toasted coconut strips.

~.~.~.~.~.~.~.~.~.~

*COOK'S TIP*
To make toasted coconut
strips, remove all the bark and
skin and cut pieces of coconut
into paper-thin slices about
5cm/2in long. Spread the slices
on a baking sheet and toast in a
preheated 170°C/325°F/Gas 3
oven until lightly browned.
Sprinkle with salt,
if you wish.

~.~.~.~.~.~.~.~.~.~

# GARDEN VEGETABLE CHOWDER

The crispy onion garnish gives a pleasant contrast to the creaminess of the soup, but it is equally good topped with grated Cheddar cheese.

**SERVES 6–8**

25g • 1oz butter
1 onion, chopped
1 shallot, chopped
1 leek, split lengthwise and
    thinly sliced
1–2 garlic cloves, minced
25g • 1oz plain flour
3 carrots, halved lengthwise
    and thinly sliced
½ small celery root, finely
    diced, or 2 celery sticks,
    finely sliced
2 small turnips, finely diced
2 large baking potatoes, diced

750ml • 1¼ pt vegetable or
    light chicken stock
bouquet garni (thyme and
    marjoram sprigs, parsley
    stems and bay leaf)
salt and white pepper
115g • 4oz chopped green beans
kernels cut from 2 cobs of corn
400ml • 14fl oz milk
175ml • 6fl oz whipping cream
crispy fried onions (see page
    124), or grated Cheddar
    cheese, to garnish

❶ Melt the butter in a large heavy saucepan over medium heat. Add the onion, shallot, leek, and garlic. Cook until the vegetables start to soften, about 5 minutes, stirring frequently. Stir in the flour and cook for 2 minutes. Add the carrots, celery root or celery, turnips, potatoes and stock, stirring and scraping the bottom of the pan.

❷ Bring to the boil, stirring frequently. Add the bouquet garni and season with salt and pepper. Simmer over medium-low heat, stirring occasionally, until the vegetables are almost tender, about 20 minutes.

❸ Stir in the beans, corn and milk. Continue cooking until the beans are tender, about 10 minutes. Stir in the cream, adjust the seasoning and heat through. Ladle into warmed bowls and garnish with crispy fried onions.

# WILD MUSHROOM SOUP

This soup gets a flavour boost from the minced mushroom base, or *duxelles*, one of the basic building blocks of French cooking. If wild mushrooms are not available, use the most flavourful domestic mushrooms you can find.

**SERVES 4**

225g • 8oz wild mushrooms or cultivated wild varieties (porcini, oyster or shiitake), wiped or rinsed and blotted dry
450g • 1lb button mushrooms, wiped or rinsed and blotted dry
25g • 1oz butter
2 shallots, finely chopped
1 garlic clove, chopped
salt and freshly ground pepper
1.5l • 2¾pt beef or brown chicken stock
2tbs plain flour
2–3tbs Cognac or brandy
bouquet garni (thyme and marjoram sprigs, parsley stems and bay leaf)
¼tsp grated nutmeg
120ml • 4fl oz whipping cream
chopped fresh chives, to garnish

❶ Cut the stems of the wild mushrooms level with the caps. Thinly slice the wild mushroom caps and set aside, and put the stems in a food processor fitted with a steel blade. Add the button mushrooms to the processor and pulse until finely chopped. (They should look like fine breadcrumbs.)

❷ Melt half the butter in a non-stick frying pan over medium heat and cook the shallots until just softened, 2–3 minutes. Add the chopped mushrooms and garlic. Continue cooking, stirring frequently, until the mushrooms have rendered and re-absorbed their liquid and are almost completely dry and starting to brown, about 10 minutes. Season with salt and pepper. Transfer to a blender, add a quarter of the stock and blend until smooth. (Blending improves the texture, but can be omitted.)

❸ Melt the remaining butter in a saucepan over medium heat, add the mushroom caps and cook for 4–5 minutes, or until they are lightly browned. Sprinkle over the flour and cook for 2–3 minutes, stirring frequently, until well blended.

❹ Stir in the Cognac and remaining stock. Add the bouquet garni and the blended mushroom and stock mixture. Simmer, covered, over low heat for 20–30 minutes, stirring occasionally.

❺ Just before serving, remove the bouquet garni, stir in the cream and cook for 1–2 minutes to heat through. Ladle into a warmed tureen or soup bowls and sprinkle with chives.

# SWEET POTATO *and* LEEK SOUP

This soup is wonderfully smooth and creamy with an elusive flavour that is hard to identify. If you are able to find sweet potatoes with pale yellow flesh and a consistency more like white potatoes than yams, omit the white potato from this recipe.

**SERVES 6**

15g • ½oz butter
4 medium leeks (about 350g • 12oz), thinly sliced
800g • 1¾lb sweet potatoes, peeled and cubed
1 medium white potato, cubed
1l • 1¾pt water
salt and freshly ground pepper
freshly grated nutmeg
600ml • 1pt chicken stock
150ml • ¼pt whipping cream
3tbsp finely chopped fresh chives

❶ Melt the butter in a large, heavy saucepan over medium-low heat. Add the leeks, cover and cook for 6–8 minutes, or until softened.
❷ Add the sweet potatoes, white potato and water. Season lightly with salt, pepper and nutmeg. Bring to the boil over high heat. Reduce the heat to medium-low and simmer, partially covered, for about 20 minutes until the vegetables are very tender, stirring occasionally.
❸ Transfer the vegetables and cooking liquid to a blender or a food processor fitted with a steel blade and purée until smooth, working in batches if necessary. Strain the mixture back into the saucepan, pressing firmly with the back of a spoon to extract as much liquid as possible. Stir in the stock, set over low heat and simmer for 10–15 minutes, or until heated through. Taste and adjust the seasoning.
❹ Using an electric mixer or whisk, whip the cream with a pinch of salt until soft peaks form. Stir in the chives.
❺ Ladle the soup into warmed bowls or soup plates and garnish with the chive-flavoured whipped cream.

# CORN CHOWDER

Both corn and potatoes originated in South America and found their way to other parts of the world via North America. Dried corn was used for this soup in the days before modern agriculture and transportation ensured the availability of fresh corn all year. This recipe is quite rich; if you prefer, use more milk instead of the cream.

**SERVES 4–6**

15g • ½oz butter
75g • 3oz thick-cut lean smoked back bacon, finely chopped
1 onion, finely chopped
450g • 1lb potatoes, diced
750ml • 1¼pt water
salt and freshly ground pepper
4 corn cobs
175ml • 6fl oz whipping cream
120ml • 4fl oz milk

❶ Melt the butter in a large heavy saucepan over medium-high heat. Add the bacon and onion, and cook, stirring frequently, until the onion is soft and the bacon golden, about 7 minutes.
❷ Add the potatoes and water, and season lightly with salt and pepper. Reduce the heat to medium-low and simmer, partially covered, until the potatoes are just tender, about 15 minutes.
❸ Cut the kernels from the corn, without cutting down to the cob. With the back of a knife, scrape the cobs to extract the milky liquid from the base of kernels. Alternatively, use a corn scraper to remove the kernels and the liquid in one process.
❹ Add the corn and its liquid to the saucepan with the cream and continue cooking for about 10 minutes, until all the vegetables are tender. Stir in the milk, adding more if needed to thin the soup to the preferred consistency. Simmer for 2–3 minutes until heated through. Taste and adjust the seasoning and ladle into a warmed tureen or bowls.

# CARAMELIZED ONION SOUP *with* CORNMEAL FRITTERS

This rich flavourful soup is based on the classic onion soup served in France, which is served with a croûton covered with grated cheese and toasted until brown and bubbly. These small cornmeal fritters are lighter and make an unusual garnish.

**SERVES 4**

| | |
|---|---|
| *15g • ½oz butter* | CORNMEAL FRITTERS |
| *4tsp olive oil* | *175ml • 6fl oz water* |
| *800g • 1¾lb large yellow* | *1 egg* |
| *onions, thinly sliced* | *75g • 3oz cornmeal* |
| *1 garlic clove, finely chopped* | *salt and freshly ground black* |
| *¼tsp sugar* | *pepper* |
| *salt* | *25g • 1oz freshly grated* |
| *20g • ¾oz plain flour* | *Parmesan cheese* |
| *150ml • ¼pt dry white wine* | *1tbsp finely chopped chives or* |
| *1.2l • 2pt beef stock* | *spring onion tops* |
| | *oil, for frying* |

❶ In a large heavy saucepan or flameproof casserole, melt the butter and olive oil over medium-low heat. Add the onions and cook, covered, for 10–12 minutes until they soften, stirring occasionally. Add the garlic, sugar and a pinch of salt, and continue cooking, uncovered, for 45–55 minutes, or until the onions turn a deep, golden brown, stirring occasionally until they start to colour, then more frequently.

❷ Stir in the flour until it is absorbed and cook for 2 minutes. Add the wine and a quarter of the stock, and bring to the boil, scraping the bottom of the pan and stirring until smooth. Add the remaining stock, reduce the heat to medium-low and simmer gently, partially covered, for 30 minutes.

❸ For the fritters, preheat the oven to 200°C/400°F/Gas 6. Put the water in a small bowl and beat in the egg. Slowly whisk in the cornmeal until smoothly blended. Season generously with salt and pepper, and stir in half the cheese and the chives. Set a large frying pan over medium-high heat and add enough oil to film the bottom of the pan. When it starts to smoke, drop the batter by scant tablespoonfuls, stirring it frequently. Cook the fritters until bubbles appear at the edges, about 1–1½ minutes, then turn over and cook for about 1 minute longer until evenly browned. Drain on paper towels and continue cooking in batches. Place the fritters on a baking sheet and sprinkle with the remaining cheese. Bake at the top of the oven until the cheese is melted.

❹ Ladle the hot soup into warmed bowls or soup plates and garnish each with three or four fritters.

~·~·~·~·~·~·~·~·~·~

*TO DRINK*
A young but full-bodied red wine, such as Côtes-du-Rhone from France or Dâo from Portugal.

~·~·~·~·~·~·~·~·~·~

# SPICY BLACK BEAN SOUP

This soup has its roots in Cuba, but shows the influence of contemporary chefs and the excitement of the food scene in Florida today.

**SERVES 4–6**

*450g • 1lb black beans (turtle or kidney)*
*1tbsp olive oil*
*2 red onions, finely chopped*
*4 garlic cloves, minced*
*75ml • 5tbsp brandy*
*2l • 3½pt water*
*bouquet garni (bay leaf, thyme and marjoram sprigs, coriander and parsley stems and 2–3 strips orange zest)*
*½tsp cumin seeds*
*¼tsp dried oregano*

*3–4 roasted ancho chilli peppers, deseeded and chopped, or 3.75ml • ¾tsp chilli flakes*
*1 tbsp concentrated tomato paste*
*3 tomatoes, peeled, seeded and chopped*
*salt and freshly ground pepper*
*6tbsp soured cream*
*3–4 spring onions, finely chopped*
*fresh coriander leaves, to garnish*

❶ Pick over the beans to remove any small stones. Cover with cold water and leave to soak for 6 hours or overnight.
❷ Drain the beans, put into a saucepan with cold water to cover and set over high heat. Bring to the boil and boil for 10 minutes. Drain and rinse well.
❸ Heat the oil in a large heavy saucepan over medium-high heat, add the onions and cook until they are just softened, 3–4 minutes, stirring frequently. Add the garlic and continue cooking for 2 minutes. Add the brandy, water, bouquet garni, cumin seeds, oregano and chillies. When the mixture begins to bubble, stir in the tomato paste, reduce the heat to low and simmer gently, partially covered, for 1½–2½ hours until the beans are tender, stirring occasionally. Remove and discard the bouquet garni and season with salt and, if necessary, pepper.
❹ Ladle the soup into a warmed tureen or bowls and top with a dollop of soured cream. Sprinkle with the spring onions and garnish with coriander leaves.

~.~.~.~.~.~.~.~.~.~

*To Drink*
Mexican beer.

~.~.~.~.~.~.~.~.~.~

# CREAM *of* ASPARAGUS SOUP

The best asparagus for soup has large stalks and tightly closed tips. At the end of the season you can often find large quantities at reasonable prices – a good time to make this soup.

**SERVES 6–8**

*1.5kg • 3lb fresh asparagus, woody ends removed*
*25g • 1oz butter*
*1 small onion, chopped*
*1.5l • 2¾pt chicken stock*
*salt and freshly ground pepper*

*120ml • 4fl oz whipping cream*
*15g • ½oz cornflour, blended with 3tbsp cold water*
*nasturtium flowers or shavings of Parmesan cheese, to garnish*

❶ Cut the asparagus into 2.5-cm/1-inch pieces. Melt the butter in a large heavy saucepan over medium-high heat. Add the onion and the asparagus pieces, and cook for 5–6 minutes, stirring frequently, until the asparagus is bright green; do not allow the pieces to brown.

❷ Stir in the stock and bring to the boil over high heat, skimming off any foam that rises to the surface. Reduce the heat to medium and simmer for about 5 minutes until the tips are just tender. Using a slotted spoon, remove 12–16 asparagus tips for garnish. Set aside, covered. Season the soup with salt and pepper, cover and continue cooking for 15–20 minutes until the asparagus stalks are very tender.

❸ Transfer the vegetables and some of the cooking liquid to a blender or a food processor fitted with a steel blade and purée until smooth, working in batches if necessary. Strain the mixture back into the saucepan, pressing firmly with the back of a spoon to extract as much liquid as possible. Bring back to the boil over medium-high heat and stir in the cream. Stir the cornflour mixture, whisk into the boiling soup and boil for 1–2 minutes until slightly thickened. Taste and adjust the seasoning.

❹ Ladle the soup into warmed bowls and garnish with the reserved asparagus tips and nasturtium flowers or Parmesan shavings.

~.~.~.~.~.~.~.~.~.~

*TO DRINK*
A fresh, fruity
Chardonnay or Pinot
Grigio.

~.~.~.~.~.~.~.~.~.~

# CHESTNUT *and* APPLE SOUP

This autumnal soup captures the flavours of the harvest – perfect as a starter at Christmas. For a more exotic, spicy soup, replace the sage with a cinnamon stick.

**SERVES 4–6**

450g • 1lb shelled, skinned chestnuts
25g • 1oz butter
1 large onion, chopped
2 medium carrots, thinly sliced
2 medium dessert apples, peeled, cored and finely chopped
1l • 1¾pt water

bouquet garni (bay leaf, 2 sage leaves, thyme sprigs and parsley stems)
salt and pepper
4tbsp single cream, or as needed
sage leaves and chives, to garnish (optional)

❶ Put the chestnuts in a saucepan, add water to cover and simmer over medium heat until chestnuts are just tender, 12–15 minutes. Remove from the heat and set aside.

❷ Melt the butter in a large heavy saucepan over medium-high heat, add the onion and carrots, and cook until the onion is just softened, about 5 minutes, stirring frequently. Add the apples, water, bouquet garni and chestnuts with their cooking liquid. Season with salt and pepper, and bring to the boil. Reduce the heat and simmer until all the vegetables are tender, about 25 minutes. Remove the bouquet garni.

❸ Transfer the solids to a blender or a food processor fitted with a metal blade, add some of the liquid and purée until smooth. Return to the saucepan, add the cream and simmer over low heat for a few minutes until heated through. Taste and adjust the seasoning. Ladle into a warmed tureen or soup plates. If you like, garnish with sage leaves and chives on the edge of the plates.

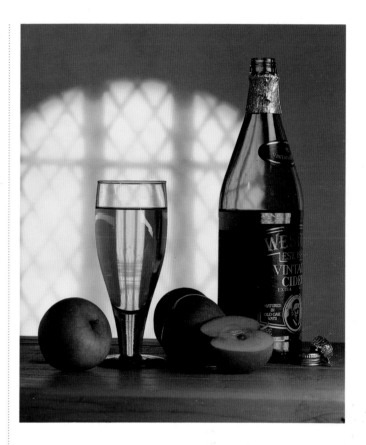

~.~.~.~.~.~.~.~.~.~.~.~

*TO DRINK*
An oaky Chardonnay or sparkling dry cider.

*COOK'S TIP*
To shell and skin chestnuts, use a small sharp knife to cut an "X" in the bottom of each chestnut. Bring a saucepan of water to the boil, add the chestnuts and boil for 6–8 minutes. Remove a few chestnuts at a time with a slotted spoon. Holding them in a towel or wearing rubber gloves, remove the shell with the aid of a paring knife, then peel off the inner skin.

~.~.~.~.~.~.~.~.~.~.~

# CHEESE *and* CELERY BISQUE

This smooth soup makes a rich but light beginning to any number of menus. The recipe calls for Cheddar cheese, but try Stilton instead for a change of pace, especially during the holiday season.

**SERVES 4**

25g • 1oz butter
1 large carrot, finely chopped
4 large celery sticks, finely chopped
1 medium onion, finely chopped
1l • 1¾pt chicken stock
bouquet garni (thyme and marjoram sprigs, parsley stems and bay leaf)
120ml • 4fl oz whipping cream
175g • 6oz grated Cheddar cheese
salt (if needed) and pepper
freshly grated nutmeg
celery leaves, to garnish

❶ Melt the butter in a heavy saucepan over medium-high heat. Add the carrot, celery and onion, and cook, stirring occasionally, until the vegetables are slightly softened, about 5 minutes. Add the stock and bouquet garni, bring to the boil, reduce the heat to low and simmer for 30 minutes.
❷ Strain the soup, pressing firmly with the back of a spoon to extract as much liquid as possible. Discard the solids and return the soup to the pan. Stir in the cream, set over low heat and simmer for 5 minutes. Slowly add the cheese, stirring constantly until smooth. Taste and adjust the seasoning, adding salt only if needed, and pepper to taste. (Do not allow the soup to boil.)
❸ Ladle into warmed serving bowls or soup plates, grate a little nutmeg over each and garnish with celery leaves.

~.~.~.~.~.~.~.~.~.~

*VARIATION*
If preferred, substitute
150g/5oz grated Stilton
cheese for the Cheddar.

*TO DRINK*
Lightly chilled
tawny port.

~.~.~.~.~.~.~.~.~.~

# CELERY ROOT *and* FENNEL SOUP

This combination of winter vegetables has a fresh, intriguing, slightly sweet flavour that is difficult to identify.

**SERVES 4–6**

15g • ½oz butter
1 leek, split lengthwise and thinly sliced
1 small onion, chopped
1 small fennel bulb, chopped
1 large celery root (about 800g • 1¾lb), peeled and cubed
1 medium potato, cubed
1.5l • 2¾pt water
salt and white pepper
bouquet garni (2–3 sprigs thyme and/or marjoram and 1 bay leaf)
175ml • 6fl oz milk, or more if needed
freshly grated nutmeg
fennel fronds, to garnish

❶ Melt the butter in a large heavy saucepan over medium heat. Add the leek, onion and fennel, and cook, stirring frequently, until just softened, about 4 minutes. Add the celery root, potato and water. Season with a little salt and add the bouquet garni. Bring to the boil over medium heat and boil gently until the vegetables are very tender, about 45 minutes.
❷ Remove the bouquet garni and transfer the solids to a blender or a food processor fitted with a steel blade. Add some of the cooking liquid and purée until smooth, working in batches if necessary.
❸ Return to the saucepan and stir in the milk, adding more if needed to thin the soup to the preferred consistency. Season to taste with salt, pepper and nutmeg. Reheat gently over low heat. Ladle into warmed bowls and garnish with fennel fronds.

~.~.~.~.~.~.~.~.~.~

*TO DRINK*
Dry Oloroso sherry.

~.~.~.~.~.~.~.~.~.~

# WILD RICE *and* WILD MUSHROOM CHOWDER

The dried mushrooms intensify the earthy flavour of the wild rice in this soup. Wild rice, which is actually an aquatic grass, is indigenous to North America and is still harvested by the native peoples of the US and Canada.

**SERVES 4–6**

| | |
|---|---|
| *50g • 2oz dried wild mushrooms (ceps or porcinis), rinsed if sandy* | *parsley stems and bay leaf)* |
| *475g • 16fl oz hot water* | *25g • 1oz butter* |
| *1l • 1¾pt chicken stock* | *2 shallots, finely chopped* |
| *150g • 5oz wild rice, rinsed in cold running water and drained* | *3 tbsp Cognac or dry sherry* |
| *bouquet garni (thyme sprigs,* | *salt and freshly ground pepper* |
| | *6tbsp whipping cream* |
| | *1tbsp finely chopped thyme leaves* |

❶ Put the dried mushrooms in a bowl, add the water and leave to soak for 10 minutes. Strain the mushroom liquid through a sieve lined with a layer of damp muslin into a saucepan. Squeeze or press the liquid from the mushrooms and reserve them. Add the stock, wild rice and bouquet garni to the mushroom liquid. Bring to the boil, reduce the heat to medium-low and simmer, partially covered, until the rice is soft and has completely split open, about 1½ hours.

❷ Strain the rice over a large bowl. Put the rice in a blender or a food processor fitted with a steel blade, add about a quarter of the cooking liquid and purée until smooth.

❸ Chop the mushrooms finely. Melt the butter in a large saucepan over medium-high heat. Add the shallots and mushrooms and cook until the shallots are soft and starting to colour, 5–7 minutes. Stir in the remaining cooking liquid, Cognac or sherry and puréed rice. Season to taste with salt and pepper, and, if you wish, thin the soup with a little more stock or water. Bring to the boil, reduce the heat to low and simmer for about 5 minutes, or until heated through.

❹ Combine the cream and thyme in a small saucepan and set over low heat until bubbles appear around the edge. Ladle the soup into warmed bowls or soup plates and swirl in the cream, dividing it evenly.

# SESAME CARROT *and* PARSNIP SOUP

The subtle Oriental overtones in this soup elevate it from ordinary to exciting.

**SERVES 4–6**

| | |
|---|---|
| 15g • ½oz butter | salt and freshly ground pepper |
| 1 onion, chopped | zest of ½ orange (unwaxed or |
| 1 leek, split and sliced | scrubbed) |
| 450g • 1lb carrots, sliced | ¼tsp Oriental sesame oil, or |
| 2 medium parsnips, peeled and | to taste |
| sliced | 750ml • 1¼pt chicken or |
| 1–2 garlic cloves, minced | vegetable stock |
| 750ml • 1¼pt water | SESAME CROUTONS |
| 7–8 coriander seeds | 3 thin slices white or wholemeal |
| 1–2 cardamom pods | bread, crusts removed |
| ¼tsp fresh thyme leaves, or | soft butter, for spreading |
| ¼tsp dried thyme | 2tbsp sesame seeds |

❶ Melt the butter in a large saucepan over medium heat and add the onion and leek. Cook until just softened, about 5 minutes, stirring occasionally. Add the carrots, parsnips, garlic and water. Tie the spices and thyme in a piece of muslin and add to the soup with a little salt and pepper. Bring to the boil, reduce the heat to low and simmer gently, partially covered, until the vegetables are tender, about 45 minutes.

❷ Transfer the vegetables and cooking liquid to a blender or a food processor fitted with a steel blade and purée until smooth. Return to the saucepan, add the orange zest, sesame oil and stock, and simmer over very low heat, stirring occasionally.

❸ For the croutons, preheat the oven to 190°C/375°F/Gas 5. Spread the bread lightly with butter, sprinkle with sesame seeds and lightly press them into the butter to help them to adhere. Cut each piece of bread diagonally into four triangles, then cut each triangle in half to form two smaller triangles. Place them on a baking sheet and bake until pale golden and crispy, about 15 minutes.

❹ Ladle the soup into warmed soup plates and top with croutons, dividing them evenly.

# ROASTED TOMATO SOUP *with* GOAT'S CHEESE CROUTONS

Roasting the tomatoes and other vegetables gives this soup added flavour, essential if using winter tomatoes.

**SERVES 4**

| | |
|---|---|
| 2 garlic cloves, finely chopped | GOAT'S CHEESE CROUTONS |
| ¼tsp each dried thyme and | 4 slices French bread |
| marjoram | 75g • 3oz firm goat's cheese |
| 3–4tbsp olive oil | (slightly smaller in diameter |
| 900g • 2lb ripe tomatoes, cored | than the bread), cut in |
| and thickly sliced | 4 slices |
| 1 medium onion, chopped | |
| salt and freshly ground pepper | |
| 300ml • ½pt vegetable or | |
| poultry stock | |

❶ Preheat the oven to 190°C/375°F/Gas 5. Mix together the garlic and herbs. Drizzle a tablespoonful of the olive oil in the bottom of a large shallow baking dish. Layer the tomatoes, onions and garlic-herb mixture in two or three layers. Drizzle each layer as you go with the olive oil and season with a little salt and pepper. Bake, uncovered, for 25 minutes, or until all the vegetables are softened.

❷ Work the vegetables through a food mill fitted with a fine blade set over a saucepan. Skim off any standing oil. Add the stock or water and simmer over medium heat, stirring occasionally, for about 15 minutes, or until heated through. Taste and adjust the seasoning, if necessary.

❸ For the goat's cheese croutons, preheat the grill. Toast the bread lightly on both sides under the grill. Top with slices of goat's cheese and grill until lightly browned.

❹ Ladle the soup into warmed shallow bowls and place a crouton in each.

~.~.~.~.~.~.~.~.~.~

*TO DRINK*
A fruity red wine,
such as Beaujolais or
other Gamay wine.

~.~.~.~.~.~.~.~.~.~

# CHAPTER TWO

# Meat Soups

MEAT SOUPS EVOKE SOME OF OUR MOST BELOVED CULINARY TRADITIONS – THE CAULDRON SUSPENDED IN THE CHIMNEY OVER THE GLOWING LOGS, THE STOCKPOT SIMMERING ON THE BACK OF THE WOOD-FIRED STOVE. RICH AROMAS WAFTING THROUGH THE AIR STIR OUR SENSES AND REKINDLE OUR APPETITE FOR ONE OF MAN'S FAVOURITE FOODS THROUGH THE AGES. FULFILLING IN MANY WAYS, SOUP WARMS THE HEART AS WELL AS THE STOMACH.

# MEAT SOUPS

Nourishing meat soups are found in many cuisines around the world from the Far East to the Middle East to Europe to the Americas. Slow cooking is the common theme and cooking meat in liquid is one of the best ways to tenderize it. Long-simmered soups and stews produce a very rich broth. Pot au feu, *one of the cornerstones of French home cooking, is the classic example but it has its counterparts in most other countries.*

*Meat soups are often economical, as inexpensive cuts respond best to this treatment and also have more flavour. They usually contain other ingredients, such as vegetables or pulses, which give them more substance and stretch them, so a little meat goes a long way.*

*Leftover meat can be used to good advantage in some soups. Substitute it in recipes in which there are plenty of other ingredients to flavour the liquid, such as tomatoes or vegetables, and add any juices or gravy.*

Stock made using bones benefits from long simmering to extract the gelatine from the bones, but soups and stocks made with boneless meat are faster. Cut the meat and vegetables into small pieces so they can yield their goodness and flavour quickly.

~.~.~.~.~.~.~.~.~.~

*"Meaty jelly, too, especially when a
little salt, which is the case when there's
ham, is mellering to the organ."*

OUR MUTUAL FRIEND
*Charles Dickens, 1812–70*

~.~.~.~.~.~.~.~.~.~

Meat stock takes longer to make than other stocks because slow
simmering is needed to extract the gelatine from the bones and
develop a rich flavour, but you can make large batches and store it
in the freezer. An acceptable short-cut stock, taking only an hour,
can be made without bones by using finely chopped vegetables and
meat. Some of the following recipes use this technique, making the
stock and the soup at the same time.

The soups in this selection offer much variety. Some are light and
elegant, like Vintner's Oxtail Soup or Poached Beef and Vegetable
Soup, some rich and aromatic, such as Italian Sausage and
Courgette Soup, some thick and satisfying, for instance, Arab
Lamb and Chickpea Soup or Texan Chilli.

# ARAB LAMB *and* CHICK-PEA SOUP

## *(Harira)*

Redolent of exotic Middle Eastern spices, this soup, a slightly tamed version of the Moroccan mutton soup *harira*, is satisfying and unusual. Lentils, dried beans or pasta are sometimes added for an even more substantial soup and in Morocco, dates are offered as an accompaniment.

**SERVES 4–6**

*115g • 4oz chick-peas, soaked overnight and drained, or 200g • 7oz canned chick-peas, rinsed and drained*
*4–6tsp olive oil*
*675g • 1½lb boneless lamb shoulder, trimmed of all fat and cut into 2.5-cm • 1-in cubes*
*1 onion, finely chopped*
*3 garlic cloves, minced*
*4tbsp dry white wine (optional)*
*1.2l • 2pt water*
*¾tsp dried thyme*
*¾tsp dried oregano*
*bay leaf*
*¼tsp ground cinnamon*
*¼tsp cumin seeds*
*4 tomatoes, peeled, deseeded and chopped, or 250ml • 8fl oz tomato juice*
*2 roasted red peppers, peeled, deseeded and chopped*
*¼tsp ground saffron or turmeric*
*1 large leek, halved lengthwise and sliced*
*1 large carrot, diced*
*1 large potato, diced*
*2 medium courgettes, halved lengthwise and sliced*
*115g • 4oz fresh or thawed frozen green peas*
*harissa (hot red pepper paste), to taste*
*chopped fresh mint leaves, to garnish*
*chopped fresh coriander leaves, to garnish*

❶ If using dried chick-peas, cook over medium heat in boiling unsalted water to cover generously until tender, about 1½ hours. Drain.

❷ Heat the oil in a flameproof casserole or large heavy saucepan over high heat. Add enough of the lamb to cover the base of the pan sparsely and cook, stirring frequently, until evenly browned. Remove the browned meat and continue cooking in batches, adding a little more oil if needed. When the last batch is nearly browned, add the onion and garlic, and cook, stirring frequently, for 2 minutes. Return all the meat to the pan and add the wine, if using, water, thyme, oregano, bay leaf, cinnamon and cumin. Bring just to the boil, skimming off any foam that rises to the surface, reduce the heat to low and simmer for about 1½ hours until the meat is very tender. Discard the bay leaf.

❸ Stir in the chick-peas, tomatoes or tomato juice, roasted peppers, saffron or turmeric, leek, carrot and potato, and simmer for 15 minutes. Add the courgettes and peas, and continue simmering for 15–20 minutes more, or until all the vegetables are tender. Taste and adjust the seasoning, adding a little harissa, if you like a spicier soup.

❹ Ladle the soup into a warmed tureen or bowls and sprinkle with mint and/or coriander.

# GEORGIAN SPICY BEEF SOUP
## *with* PLUMS

*Kharcho*, this slightly sour soup from the former Soviet Union, appears in many versions. It is often flavoured with dried plums, but fresh plums add the needed tartness and are easier to find. Fenugreek is essential for authenticity, but its unusual taste is not pleasing to everyone and it can be difficult to obtain. Do not hesitate to try the soup with or without it.

**SERVES 6**

4 garlic cloves
5 allspice berries
10 peppercorns
15 coriander seeds
½tsp fenugreek seeds
½tsp dried chilli flakes
900g • 2lb boneless stewing beef, cut in 2.5-cm • 1-in cubes
2 onions, finely chopped
1 carrot, finely chopped
large bouquet garni (2 bay leaves, coriander and parsley stems, thyme and savory sprigs and celery leaves
2.5l • 4½pt water
2tsp vegetable oil

2 garlic cloves, minced
6 tomatoes, preferably plum, peeled, deseeded and chopped
6 large plums, stoned, peeled and finely chopped
½tsp dried summer savory
½tsp dried fenugreek leaves, crushed
¼tsp turmeric
¼tsp hot paprika, or a pinch of cayenne pepper
salt
lemon juice, to taste
1–2tbsp plum preserves (optional)
3tbsp chopped fresh coriander leaves, to garnish

❶ Lightly crush 2 of the garlic cloves and put them in a piece of muslin with the allspice berries, peppercorns, coriander and fenugreek seeds, and dried chilli flakes. Tie with string.

❷ Put the cubes of beef in a flameproof casserole or large saucepan with half the onions and the carrot. Add the bouquet garni, spice bag and water. Bring to the boil over medium-high heat, skimming off any foam that rises to the surface. Reduce the heat to low and simmer, partially covered, for 1½–2 hours until the meat is very tender, skimming as necessary and stirring occasionally.

❸ Strain the cooking liquid and discard the vegetables, bouquet garni and spice bag. Remove the meat from the bones and discard the fat, cartilage and bones. Spoon off the fat from the cooking liquid. (If preparing the recipe in advance, chill the meat until needed. Cool the cooking liquid and chill, covered; remove the fat when it is congealed and hard.)

❹ Heat the oil in a large saucepan, add the remaining onions and cook over medium heat until just softened, about 3 minutes. Add the garlic, tomatoes, plums, savory, dried fenugreek, turmeric, paprika or cayenne and a little salt, and continue cooking for 5 minutes, stirring frequently. Add the beef and its cooking liquid, bring back to the boil, reduce the heat to low and simmer for about 45 minutes, stirring occasionally.

❺ Taste and adjust the seasoning and stir in a few drops of lemon juice, or as needed, and if you wish, the plum preserves. (The soup should be slightly sour.) Ladle into warmed bowls and sprinkle with coriander leaves.

# POACHED BEEF *and* VEGETABLE SOUP

*(Boeuf à la nage)*

This elegant soup is a sophisticated and speedy version of *pot au feu*, the long-simmered classic of French country cooking. Select very small vegetables or cut larger ones into sticks or other small bite-size shapes. The stock should be rich and flavourful: reduce weak stock to concentrate the flavour before using.

**SERVES 4**

| | |
|---|---|
| 1l • 1¾pt beef stock | 16 small button mushrooms |
| 1–2tbsp dry sherry or red wine | 1 baby cabbage, quartered |
| 350g • 12oz beef fillet, about | 6 dwarf squash, halved |
|   6cm • 2½in thick, tied | 16 sugar snap peas |
| 16 tiny dwarf carrots | 1tbsp chopped fresh parsley |
| 12–16 tiny new potatoes | 1tbsp chopped fresh chives |

❶ In a medium saucepan, bring the stock to the boil, add the sherry or wine and reduce the heat to medium-low. Add the beef, carrots, potatoes and mushrooms, and simmer for 5 minutes. Add the cabbage and continue cooking for 7 minutes. Add the squash and peas, and continue cooking for 4–5 minutes.

❷ Transfer the meat to a chopping board. Test the vegetables to make sure they are cooked, as cooking time varies slightly depending on their size. Continue simmering if they are not cooked. Remove the vegetables and bring the stock to the boil.

❸ Cut the meat in half lengthwise and slice each half into pieces about 3mm/⅛in thick. (It should be very rare, as it will continue cooking in the stock.) Divide the meat among warmed shallow soup plates or bowls and arrange the vegetables evenly. Ladle over the boiling stock and sprinkle with herbs.

~.~.~.~.~.~.~.~.~

TO DRINK
A medium-bodied
*cru bourgeois* red
Bordeaux.

~·~·~·~·~·~·~·~·~

# PORK *and* HOMINY SOUP

*(Posole)*

Dried corn kernels treated with lime to soften the outer hull are known as hominy, or in the south west of the US, posole. The process, which improves the nutritional value of the grain, goes back to the Mayans and Aztecs, native civilizations of South America. Canned hominy may be used if the dried variety is not available. Sometimes tomatoes are omitted from the soup and tomato salsa is added at the table. The crispy vegetable garnishes provide a pleasing element of contrast.

**SERVES 4**

| | |
|---|---|
| 350g • 12oz boneless pork, cut | 1 x 400g • 14oz can chopped |
|   in 2-cm • ¾-in cubes |   canned tomatoes in juice |
| juice of 1 lime | 1–2 roasted ancho chillies, |
| 4 garlic cloves, minced |   seeds and core discarded, |
| 225g • 8oz dried corn (posole), |   chopped, or ¼tsp dried |
|   soaked for 3–12 hours, or |   chilli flakes |
|   575g • 1¼lb canned hominy, | salt |
|   rinsed and drained | TO GARNISH |
| 1tbsp rendered pork fat or | soured cream |
|   vegetable oil | shredded iceberg lettuce |
| 600ml • 1pt chicken stock | chopped spring onions |
| ¾tsp dried oregano | sliced radishes |
| ¾tsp ground cumin | lime wedges |

❶ Put the pork in a shallow glass or ceramic dish, add the lime juice and half the garlic, and stir to coat. Leave to marinate for 2–12 hours.

❷ If using dried corn, cook over medium heat in boiling unsalted water to cover generously until just tender, 1–2 hours. Drain.

❸ Strain and reserve the marinade. Scrape off and discard the garlic and pat the meat dry. Heat the fat or oil in a flame-proof casserole or large heavy saucepan over medium-high heat. Brown the meat, in batches if necessary, not crowding the pan and turning to colour evenly. When all the meat is browned, return to the pan and add the stock, oregano, cumin and the remaining garlic. Reduce the heat to low and simmer for about 45 minutes, or until the meat is tender. Stir in the tomatoes, the drained cooked or canned hominy, chillies and salt to taste. Bring to the boil, reduce the heat to low and simmer for 20–30 minutes longer.

❹ Ladle into a warmed tureen or bowls and serve with soured cream, lettuce, spring onions, radishes and lime wedges.

# RABBIT *and* LEEK SOUP *with* PRUNES

Agen is the centre of prune production in France and there you can find many dishes combining prunes with meat, poultry and even fish. Rabbit is traditionally paired with prunes; if you are able to obtain a wild rabbit, the flavour of the soup will be more robust.

**SERVES 6**

| | |
|---|---|
| *3 large leeks* | *4–5 fresh thyme sprigs, or* |
| *1tbsp vegetable oil* | *½tsp dried thyme* |
| *1kg • 2¼lb rabbit pieces* | *bay leaf* |
| *6tbsp dry white wine* | *1.5l • 2¾pt chicken stock* |
| *500ml • 18fl oz water* | *18 stoned prunes, about* |
| *3 garlic cloves, crushed* | *175g • 6oz* |
| | *salt and freshly ground pepper* |

❶ Thinly slice the white part of the leeks and reserve. Chop the green parts.

❷ Heat the oil in a large flameproof casserole over medium-high heat. Add the rabbit pieces and cook until golden brown, turning to colour evenly. Add the wine and water, bring to the boil and add the chopped green part of the leeks, garlic and herbs. Add the stock, reduce the heat to low, cover and simmer very gently for about 1 hour until the rabbit is very tender. (Wild rabbit may take longer.) Strain the cooking liquid and discard the vegetables and herbs. When cool enough to handle, take the rabbit meat from the bones.

❸ Remove as much fat as possible from the cooking liquid and put it in a large saucepan with the rabbit meat, sliced leeks and prunes. Season with salt and pepper to taste. Bring to the boil over medium-high heat, reduce the heat to low and simmer gently, stirring occasionally, until the leeks are tender. Taste and adjust the seasoning, if needed, and ladle the soup into a warmed tureen or bowls.

~.~.~.~.~.~.~.~.~

*TO DRINK*
A medium-dry fruity
rosé, especially one
from the south west
of France.

~.~.~.~.~.~.~.~.~

# VINTNERS' OXTAIL SOUP

Grapes were among the earliest cultivated plants and, while used primarily for wine, they have also featured in the kitchen, especially in medieval cooking. The contemporary fashion for combining fruit with meat, poultry or fish owes its popularity to the *nouvelle cuisine* movement of the 1970s. If you start this soup the day before, it is easy to remove all the fat from the rich stock.

**SERVES 4–6**

| | |
|---|---|
| *1.5kg • 3lb oxtails, cut in 5-cm • 2-in pieces* | *15g • ½oz butter* |
| *2 small onions, quartered* | *115g • 4oz button mushrooms, thinly sliced* |
| *2 carrots, cut in chunks* | *1 small leek, thinly sliced* |
| *4–5 garlic cloves* | *grated zest of ½ unwaxed lemon* |
| *salt and freshly ground pepper* | *150g • 5oz seedless white grapes, skinned, if wished, and halved* |
| *4tbsp dry white wine* | |
| *2.5l • 4½pt water* | |
| *large bouquet garni (parsley stems, thyme and bay leaf )* | *lemon juice, to taste (optional)* |

❶ Preheat the oven to 220°C/425°F/Gas 7. Remove as much fat as possible from the oxtails. Put them in a shallow roasting tin with the onions, carrots and garlic. Season lightly with salt and pepper, and roast, turning and stirring occasionally, for 30–40 minutes until well browned.

❷ Transfer the meat and vegetables to a large flameproof casserole or stockpot. Spoon off as much fat as possible from the roasting tin, set over high heat and add the white wine. Bring to the boil, stirring and scraping the bottom of the tin. Pour the liquid into the casserole or stockpot. Add the water and bouquet garni. Bring just to the boil, reduce the heat to low and simmer very gently, partially covered, for 3–4 hours until the meat is very tender. Using a slotted spoon, remove the oxtails. Strain the cooking liquid and discard the vegetables.

❸ Cool the cooking liquid and chill, covered. Remove the meat from the oxtails and discard the fat, cartilage and bone. Chill the meat until needed.

❹ Remove and discard the congealed fat from the cooking liquid. Melt the butter in a large saucepan over medium heat. Add the mushrooms and cook until lightly browned, about 5 minutes. Stir in the leeks and cook until just softened, about 5 minutes longer. Add the cooking liquid, lemon zest, grapes, and the reserved meat. Bring just to the boil, reduce the heat to medium-low and simmer for 10–15 minutes, or until the soup is hot and the grapes are tender. Taste and adjust the seasoning, adding a few drops of lemon juice, if wished. Ladle into warmed bowls.

~.~.~.~.~.~.~.~.~.~
*TO DRINK*
A fruity powerful
white wine, such as
Gewürztraminer.

~·~·~·~·~·~·~·~·~·~

# ITALIAN SAUSAGE *and* COURGETTE SOUP

This soup emphasizes the fennel used to flavour many Italian sausages. If other sausages are used, add a pinch of fennel seeds to the soup. The lemon, garlic and parsley seasoning, or *gremolata*, a traditional garnish for stews and seafood, brings a pleasant zing to the soup.

**SERVES 4–6**

450g • 1lb sweet Italian
   sausages
1tbsp olive oil
1 large onion, finely chopped
2 garlic cloves, minced
1 fennel bulb, finely chopped
½ red or yellow pepper,
   deseeded and finely chopped
450g • 1lb courgettes, coarsely
   grated
1.5l • 2¾pt brown chicken or
   beef stock

1tsp chopped fresh
   marjoram, or ¼tsp dried
1tsp chopped fresh thyme, or
   ¼tsp dried
bay leaf
salt and freshly ground pepper
LEMON-GARLIC SEASONING
grated zest of ½ lemon,
   unwaxed or scrubbed
1 garlic clove, minced
2tbsp chopped parsley,
   preferably flat-leafed

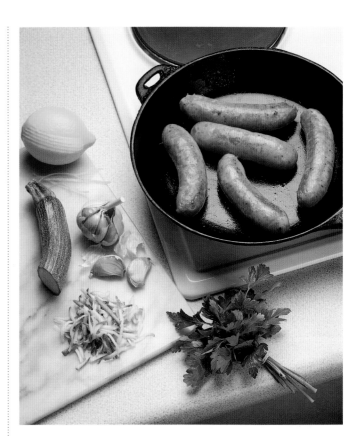

❶ Put the sausages in a frying pan and set over medium heat. Cook until well browned, turning to colour evenly. Remove and drain on paper towels. Cut into slices.
❷ Heat the oil in a heavy saucepan or flameproof casserole over medium-high heat. Add the onion, garlic, fennel and pepper, and cook for 3–4 minutes, stirring occasionally, until slightly softened.
❸ Add the courgettes, stock and herbs. Stir in the sliced sausages, reduce the heat to low and simmer for about 20 minutes. Add a little stock or water if you like a thinner soup. Season to taste with salt, if needed, and pepper. Discard the bay leaf.
❹ For the lemon-garlic seasoning, chop together the lemon zest, garlic and parsley until very fine and stir into the soup. Heat through and ladle into a warmed tureen or bowl.

~.~.~.~.~.~.~.~.~.~

*TO DRINK*
Most medium-bodied
fruity Italian red
wines, such as a good
Valpolicella.

~.~.~.~.~.~.~.~.~.~

~.~.~.~.~.~.~.~.~.~

*COOK'S TIP*
This is a good
way to use a marrow.
If the skin is very
tough, peel before
grating.

~.~.~.~.~.~.~.~.~.~

# MEATBALL SOUP *with* CABBAGE *and* PARMESAN CHEESE

These flavourful meatballs can be shaped and browned ahead, so the final preparation of the soup is easier. Make them quite small so they are really bite-sized.

**SERVES 8**

*1 large onion, halved*
*4–5tbsp olive oil*
*1 garlic clove, finely minced*
*50g • 2oz soft breadcrumbs*
*450g • 1lb lean minced*
*  beef or veal*
*1 egg, lightly beaten*
*¾tsp chopped fresh thyme*
*  leaves, or ¼tsp dried*
*¾tsp chopped fresh*
*  marjoram leaves, or*
*  ¼tsp dried*

*2tbsp freshly grated Parmesan*
*  cheese, plus more for serving*
*salt and freshly ground pepper*
*flour, for coating*
*350g • 12oz young green*
*  cabbage, cored, quartered*
*  and thinly sliced*
*800g • 1¾lb tomatoes, peeled,*
*  deseeded and chopped*
*2l • 3½pt brown chicken*
*  or beef stock*

❶ Chop half the onion finely. Slice the other half thinly and reserve. Heat 10ml/2tsp of the oil in a small frying pan over medium heat and cook the chopped onion until just softened, about 3 minutes, stirring frequently. Add the garlic and continue cooking for 2 minutes longer. Remove from the heat and leave to cool slightly.

❷ Put the breadcrumbs in a small bowl and cover with water. Leave to stand for 2 minutes, drain and squeeze dry. In a mixing bowl, combine the breadcrumbs, chopped onion, meat, egg, thyme, marjoram and Parmesan cheese. Season with salt, if needed, and plenty of pepper. Mix thoroughly and roll into small balls about 2cm/¾in in diameter. Roll the balls in flour to coat lightly.

❸ Heat 30ml/2tbsp of the remaining oil in a large frying pan over medium-high heat. Brown the meatballs in batches, not crowding the pan and turning to colour evenly. Remove and drain on paper towels. (Chill, if making in advance.)

❹ Heat the remaining oil in a large saucepan over medium heat. Add the reserved onion slices and cabbage, and cook for 3–4 minutes, stirring frequently, until they start to wilt. Add the tomatoes, stock and meatballs. Bring to the boil, reduce the heat to medium-low and simmer for about 20 minutes, or until the vegetables are tender. Taste and adjust the seasoning if necessary. Ladle into warmed bowls and serve sprinkled with Parmesan cheese.

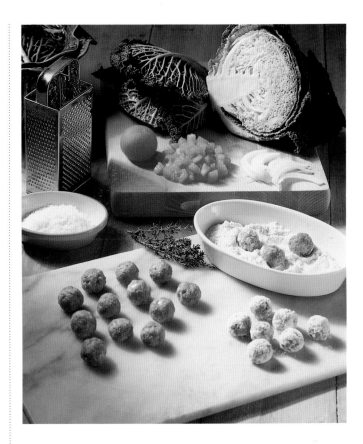

~.~.~.~.~.~.~.~.~.~

*TO DRINK*
A good
Crianza Rioja or
Chianti.

~.~.~.~.~.~.~.~.~.~

# TEXAN CHILLI

This popular style of fiery soup probably came about of necessity in a cattle drive chuckwagon. Now it offers scope for almost limitless variation. This recipe is equally good made with pork or venison instead of beef. If you like, serve cooked and seasoned kidney or pinto beans to accompany.

**SERVES 8**

*2 red peppers*
*2 fresh ancho or Jalapeño chillies*
*1.75kg • 3½lb lean beef (chuck steak)*
*3tbsp olive oil*
*2 large sweet onions, finely chopped*
*4–5 garlic cloves*
*120ml • 4fl oz red wine*
*250ml • 8fl oz tomato purée*
*750ml • 1¼pt tomato juice*

*750ml • 1¼pt beef stock, or brown chicken stock*
*250ml • 8fl oz water, or more*
*large bouquet garni (bay leaf, coriander stems and thyme)*
*1tsp cumin seeds, crushed*
*1tsp dried oregano*
*salt*
*2tsp chilli powder, or to taste*
*soured cream, to garnish*
*chopped coriander leaves, to garnish*

❶ Preheat the oven to 200°C/400°F/Gas 6. Put the peppers and chillies in a baking dish at the top of the oven and roast for about 30–40 minutes, turning a quarter turn every 10 minutes, until the peppers are wrinkly and the skin has begun to darken. Put them in a plastic storage box or bag, close tightly and leave to steam for 30 minutes. Halve the peppers and remove the cores, seeds and skin. (Wear rubber gloves when handling chillies and avoid touching eyes or other sensitive areas.) Roughly chop the pepper flesh.

❷ Chop the beef very finely with a large knife or in a food processor fitted with a steel blade, working in small batches and pulsing to avoid puréeing the meat.

❸ Heat half the oil in a large frying pan over high heat. Add enough meat to cover the bottom of the pan sparsely and cook, stirring frequently, until evenly browned. Remove the browned meat to a large non-reactive saucepan and continue cooking in batches. When all the meat is browned, reduce the heat to medium and add the onions and garlic. Cook, stirring frequently, until they start to soften, 4–5 minutes. Add the wine and boil for 1 minute, stirring and scraping the bottom of the pan to dissolve the brown bits, and pour over the meat.

❹ Stir in the peppers and chillies, tomato purée, tomato juice, stock and water, adding more if needed to cover by at least 2.5cm/1in. Add the herb bouquet, cumin, oregano and salt to taste. Bring to the boil, reduce the heat to low and simmer, partially covered, for 1 hour. Stir in the chilli powder and continue cooking for 30 minutes longer, or until the meat is very tender, stirring occasionally. Taste and adjust the seasoning, adding more chilli powder, if wished.

❺ Ladle into warmed bowls and serve garnished with soured cream and coriander leaves.

# HAM *and* SPLIT PEA SOUP

This rich, thick soup is ideal for making in advance and the ham stock gives it an intensity of flavour. If time is short, omit making ham stock, use 1l/1¾pt each water and chicken stock, and add the bouquet garni to the soup, removing it before puréeing.

**SERVES 6**

*450g • 1lb split yellow peas*
*15g • ½oz butter*
*3 shallots or 1 small onion,*
  *finely chopped*
*1 large carrot, grated*
*1 small piece celery with leaves,*
  *finely chopped*
*225g • 8oz smoked ham*
  *(gammon) steak, trimmed of*
  *all fat and cut into small*
  *pieces*
*freshly ground pepper*
*1tsp chopped fresh sage or*
  *thyme*
*3–4tbsp dry sherry (optional)*
*chopped fresh parsley, to*
  *garnish*

HAM STOCK

*675g • 1½lb ham bones (ham*
  *hock, knuckle or shank),*
  *rinsed, and a chicken*
  *carcass (or 3–4 wings)*
*1 large onion, quartered and*
  *studded with 2 cloves*
*2 large carrots, sliced*
*2 celery sticks, sliced*
*4 garlic cloves*
*5 allspice berries*
*10 peppercorns*
*bouquet garni (2 bay leaves,*
  *4–5 sage leaves, 1 small*
  *rosemary sprig, 3–4 thyme*
  *sprigs and parsley stems,*
  *tied)*
*120ml • 4fl oz dry white wine*
*3l • 5pt water*

❶ To make the stock, put the ham bones and chicken carcass in a large pot with the studded onion, carrots, celery, garlic, allspice berries, peppercorns, bouquet garni, wine and water. Bring to the boil over medium-high heat, skimming off the foam as it rises to the surface. Reduce the heat to medium-low and simmer, partially covered, for about 3½ hours until flavourful and slightly reduced.

❷ Strain the stock and discard the vegetables, spices and herbs. Remove any meat from the ham bone and cut into small pieces. Discard all fat, cartilage and bone. Spoon off the fat from the stock. (If preparing in advance, chill the meat until needed. Cool the stock and chill, covered; remove the fat when it is congealed.)

❸ Rinse the split peas under cold running water. Melt the butter in a large flameproof casserole or stockpot over medium heat. Add the shallots or onion and cook until just softened, about 3 minutes, stirring occasionally. Add the carrot and celery, and continue cooking for 2 minutes. Add

the peas, ham stock and any meat from the stock bones. Season with plenty of pepper and simmer gently for about 1 hour, or until the peas are soft.

❹ Purée the soup, in batches if necessary, in a blender or a food processor fitted with a metal blade, or pass it through a food mill fitted with a fine disc.

❺ Return the soup to a large saucepan and stir in the ham and sage or thyme. Thin with water if you like a thinner soup, and simmer gently over low heat for about 30 minutes. Stir in the sherry, if using, and heat through. Taste and adjust the seasoning. Ladle into a warmed tureen or individual soup bowls and garnish with parsley.

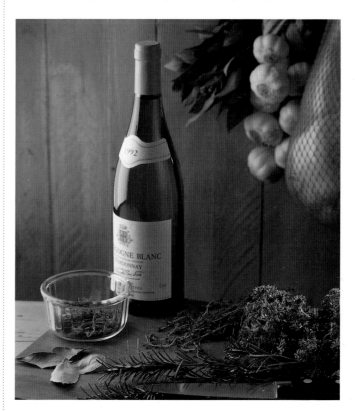

~·~·~·~·~·~·~·~·~·~

*TO DRINK*
Well chilled Fino
sherry or an oaky
white wine.

~·~·~·~·~·~·~·~·~·~

CHAPTER THREE

# Poultry and Game Soups

A N ELIXIR OF HEALTH, A COMFORTER OF
MISERIES, CHICKEN SOUP SEEMS TO HAVE
MYSTICAL PROPERTIES AND WE CONSUME IT WITH
REVERENCE AS WELL AS RELISH. WHEN IT COMES
TO GOODNESS, GAME BIRDS ARE EQUALLY WELL
SUITED FOR SOUPMAKING, WHEN SLOW SIMMERING
HIGHLIGHTS THE EXOTIC FLAVOURS AND TENDER-
IZES AT THE SAME TIME.

# POULTRY *and* GAME SOUPS

*C*hicken Soup is soothing, satisfying and invigorating. It is good either plain or fancy and its curative properties are well documented. In fact, it is sometimes known as "Jewish penicillin". The most international soup of all, it also features in Chinese, French, Spanish, Italian, Mexican, American and almost all other cuisines.

Chicken stock is used in soup-making more often than any other because it amalgamates and supports the flavours of the other ingredients, whether they are delicate, like ground almonds, or robust, like sprouting broccoli. It is quicker to cook than meat stock

and you will have the makings of two meals if you use a whole bird instead of just trimmings and bones to make the stock, providing cooked chicken for salad or casserole – or to serve in chicken soup!

Other poultry stocks are equally delicious and may be substituted for chicken stock, unless they are particularly gamey. Then they are better enjoyed on their own or with a little of the meat in them, as in Pheasant Soup.

The versatility of poultry-based

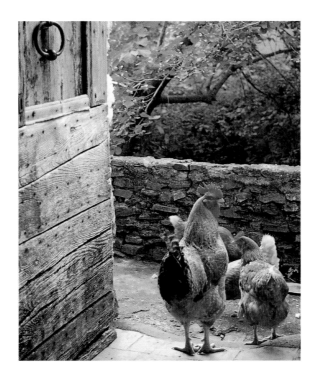

The most flavourful chicken soups are those made from mature barnyard birds – an old hen is really best. Larger birds may be tough, but in long-simmered soup, that is not a problem. Wing tips and giblets add extra flavour to poultry stocks.

*soups is limitless. They run the gamut from heartwarming traditional favourites like Chicken Soup with Herb Dumplings to novel creations such as Turkey Chilli, from foreign classics like Chinese Chicken and Corn Soup to mainstream staples like Chicken Soup with Homemade Noodles. They thrive with sultry spices or subtle seasoning, and you can change the nature of the soup by varying the ingredients you add and the garnishes you use. These are soups for all occasions to be enjoyed by everyone.*

*The potential of poultry is boundless in soup-making. Explore the possibilities offered by chicken, turkey, duck, pheasant and other game birds.*

~.~.~.~.~.~.~.~.~.~

*"Fesaunt exceedeth all foules in sweetnesse and wholesomenesse, and is equal to a capon in nourishment . . . It is meate for Princes and great estates, and for poor Schollers when they can get it."*

THE CASTEL OF HELTH
*1539, Sir Thomas Elyot*

~.~.~.~.~.~.~.~.~.~

# CHICKEN VELVET SOUP *with* ALMOND BALLS

The silky texture and elegant nature of this soup make it perfect for entertaining. A flavourful stock with all fat removed is essential. If you wish, make the almond balls a few hours beforehand and reheat them in a moderate oven for serving.

**SERVES 6**

| | |
|---|---|
| 200g • 7oz blanched whole almonds | 3 eggs, separated |
| 150ml • ¼pt milk | vegetable oil, for frying |
| 40g • 1½oz fresh white breadcrumbs | 1.5l • 2¾pt chicken stock |
| | 3tbsp cornflour |
| | 175ml • 6fl oz whipping cream |
| salt and white pepper | freshly grated nutmeg |

❶ In a food processor fitted with a steel blade, process the almonds until finely ground. Put in a small saucepan and pour over the milk. Set over medium-high heat until bubbles appear around the edge. Remove from the heat and leave to stand for 30 minutes. Strain and reserve the almonds and milk separately.

❷ To make the almond balls, combine the breadcrumbs and reserved ground almonds with a pinch of salt in a small bowl. Beat the egg whites in a shallow bowl until frothy. Stir enough of the egg whites into the almond-breadcrumb mixture to make it stick together. Form into small balls about 1cm/½in in diameter. Roll the balls in the remaining egg white and place on a wire rack until all are coated. In a frying pan, add oil to a depth of about 5mm/¼in. Heat over medium-high heat until hot. Fry the balls, a few at a time, turning to colour evenly. Drain on paper towels. Keep warm in a moderately slow oven.

❸ Combine the chicken stock and reserved almond milk in a large heavy-based saucepan and place over medium heat until it begins to tremble. In a medium bowl, whisk together the egg yolks, add the cornflour and cream and whisk until smooth. Whisk in a quarter of the hot stock mixture, then pour it all back into the saucepan, whisking constantly. With a wooden spoon, stir over medium-low heat until the soup begins to thicken, about 15 minutes (do not allow to boil or mixture may curdle). Season to taste with salt, pepper and nutmeg. Ladle into warmed shallow soup plates and garnish with almond balls.

# TURKEY *and* WILD RICE SOUP

Most turkey soups have been devised as a way of using leftover turkey, and this recipe can serve that purpose with a new twist. Try to remember to roast the garlic with the turkey, or put it in the oven to bake with something else. It needs about 30 minutes in a 200°C/400°F/Gas 6 oven and will keep refrigerated for 2–3 days. The fried sage leaves echo the holiday theme, but if you prefer, garnish with chopped fresh tarragon or parsley instead.

**SERVES 4**

| | |
|---|---|
| 1 head garlic, wrapped in foil and roasted until soft | salt and freshly ground pepper |
| 1.5l • 2¾pt turkey stock | 200g • 7oz cooked wild rice |
| 115g • 4oz oyster mushrooms, or other flavourful wild or cultivated mushrooms | 150g • 5oz chopped cooked turkey |
| | oil, for frying |
| 15g • ½oz butter | 12–16 fresh sage leaves, to garnish |

❶ Put the garlic and stock in a large saucepan over medium heat and bring to the boil slowly over medium heat. Reduce the heat to low and simmer gently, partially covered, for about 20 minutes, or until the garlic has flavoured the stock.

❷ Meanwhile, cut the mushrooms into thin strips or slices. Melt the butter in a frying pan over medium heat. Add the mushrooms, season lightly with salt and pepper, and cook, stirring gently and frequently, until lightly browned.

❸ Remove the garlic from the stock with a slotted spoon. (Don't discard; it can be used to flavour something else.) Stir in the rice, turkey and mushrooms and simmer for 10–15 minutes.

❹ Pour enough oil into a small frying pan to cover the bottom generously. Set over high heat until the oil starts to smoke. Add the sage leaves and fry until crispy, about 20 seconds. Drain on paper towels.

❺ Ladle the soup into a warmed tureen or soup bowls and garnish with the sage leaves.

# TURKEY CHILLI

Chilli comes in all colours and this green, relatively mild chilli has a creamy richness and appealing complexity.

**SERVES 6**

25g • 1oz butter
450g • 1lb skinless boneless
    turkey, finely chopped
    or minced
1 onion, finely chopped
2 celery sticks, finely chopped
1 green pepper, cored, deseeded
    and finely chopped
2 garlic cloves, minced
1 green chilli pepper, cored,
    deseeded and finely chopped

1l • 1¾pt turkey or chicken
    stock
½tsp chilli powder, or to taste
    (optional)
4tbsp extra-virgin olive oil
75g • 3oz blanched almonds
75g • 3oz stoned green olives
salt and freshly ground pepper
1 bunch parsley, stems removed

❶ Melt the butter in a flameproof casserole or large saucepan over medium heat. Add the turkey and cook, stirring frequently, until lightly browned, about 5 minutes. Stir in the onion, celery and green pepper, and cook until softened. Add the garlic and chilli pepper, and continue cooking for 2–3 minutes, stirring constantly.

❷ Stir in the stock and bring just to the boil. Reduce the heat to medium-low and simmer for 5 minutes. Taste and add chilli powder if you like it hotter.

❸ Meanwhile, put the oil, almonds, olives and half the parsley in a food processor fitted with a steel blade and process until puréed. Stir the green purée into the soup, season with salt and pepper to taste and simmer, covered, for 20 minutes.

❹ Finely chop the remaining parsley. Ladle the chilli into a warmed tureen or bowls and sprinkle with chopped parsley.

# CHINESE CHICKEN *and* CORN SOUP

This Eastern soup is appreciated around the world. The delicate flavours and subtle spicing make it an approachable and suitably light starter for entertaining, not to be reserved just for Oriental meals.

**SERVES 6**

*1.5l • 2¾pt chicken stock*
*2 boneless skinless chicken*
  *breasts*
*1 small onion, roughly chopped*
*1 carrot, roughly chopped*
*1 celery stick, roughly chopped*
*2.5-cm • 1-in piece fresh root*
  *ginger, peeled and sliced*
*bouquet garni (parsley stems,*
  *leek greens and bay leaf)*
*4 corn cobs, or 400g • 14oz*

*thawed frozen or canned*
  *corn kernels*
*3tbsp cornflour, or*
  *4tbsp if using kernels (see*
  *Cook's Tip below)*
*8 spring onions*
*salt and white pepper*
*2 egg whites, beaten with*
  *3tbsp water*
*50g • 2oz cooked ham, cut into*
  *matchstick strips*

❶ Put the stock in a large saucepan with the chicken, onion, carrot, celery, root ginger and bouquet garni. Bring to the boil over medium-high heat, skimming off any foam that rises to the surface. Reduce the heat to medium-low and simmer, partially covered, for 30–40 minutes, or until the chicken is very tender. Strain the stock, remove the chicken and discard the vegetables. Shred the chicken.

❷ Cut the kernels from the sweetcorn, without cutting down to the cob. With the back of a knife, scrape the cobs to extract the milky liquid from the base of kernels.

❸ Combine the strained stock, half the spring onions and the corn kernels and their liquid, if available, in the saucepan, and season with salt and white pepper. Bring to the boil slowly over medium heat and boil gently for 5 minutes.

❹ Stir the cornflour into 45ml/3tbsp cold water until dissolved and pour into the soup, stirring constantly. Cook, stirring, until the soup thickens, about 5 minutes. Slowly pour the egg whites into the soup while stirring vigorously. Add the ham and shredded chicken, and heat through, 1–2 minutes. Ladle into warmed bowls and garnish with the remaining spring onions.

~·~·~·~·~·~·~·~·~·~

*COOK'S TIP*
If you are using
frozen or canned corn,
it will not thicken the
soup as much as the
starchy liquid from
the corn, so increase
the cornflour to 4tbsp.

~·~·~·~·~·~·~·~·~·~

# CHICKEN SOUP *with* HERB DUMPLINGS

The secret of light dumplings is simmering them very gently on top of the liquid and not peeking. The herbs to flavour them can vary according to what you have available, but fresh herbs give the best colour and flavour.

**SERVES 6**

*1 x 1.75-kg • 4-lb chicken, quartered*
*2.5l • 4½pt water*
*2 celery sticks, sliced*
*2 carrots, sliced*
*3 shallots or 1 onion, sliced*
*2 leeks, slit lengthwise and sliced*
*2–3 garlic cloves, crushed*
*1 onion, studded with 3 cloves*
*2tsp peppercorns*
*2 allspice berries*
*large bouquet garni (parsley stems, thyme and tarragon sprigs, and bay leaf)*
*salt and freshly ground pepper*

*pinch saffron threads, soaked in 2tbsp hot water (optional)*
*40g • 1½oz butter*
*50g • 2oz plain flour*
DUMPLINGS
*115g • 4oz plain flour*
*1tsp baking powder*
*¼tsp salt*
*15g • ½oz soft butter*
*1tbsp chopped fresh parsley*
*1tbsp chopped fresh tarragon, or mixed chives and thyme*
*1 egg yolk*
*3tbsp milk*

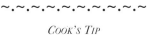

*COOK'S TIP*
To prepare in advance, cook the chicken and chill the chicken and stock separately. Remove any congealed fat from the stock and reheat gently before continuing. If making the soup all at once, the dumplings can be prepared an hour or so beforehand, while the chicken is cooking, and kept in the refrigerator, covered, until needed.

❶ Put the chicken in a large saucepan with the water, celery, carrots, shallots or onion, leeks, garlic and studded onion. Wrap the peppercorns and allspice berries in a piece of muslin and tie with string. Add the spice bag and bouquet garni with a little salt. If needed, add more water to cover the ingredients. Bring just to the boil over medium-high heat, skimming off the foam that rises to the surface. Reduce the heat to medium-low and simmer, partially covered, for about 1½ hours until the chicken is tender, skimming from time to time.

❷ Remove the chicken with a slotted spoon and set aside to cool. Add the saffron, if using, to the stock and continue simmering, uncovered. Skin the chicken and take the meat from the bones; discard the skin and bones. Cut the meat into large pieces and reserve.

❸ Remove as much fat as possible from the stock and strain into a large measuring container: there should be about 2l/3½pt. Reduce the stock if necessary. Discard the studded onion, bouquet garni and spice bag, and reserve the cooking vegetables.

❹ In a large heavy saucepan, melt the butter over medium-high heat. Stir in the flour and cook for 2–3 minutes until it starts to colour. Gradually pour in a quarter of the stock, whisking constantly. Bring to the boil, whisking, and cook for 2 minutes. Whisk in the remaining stock and when it comes back to the boil, reduce the heat to medium-low, add the reserved chicken and vegetables, and season to taste. Simmer, stirring occasionally, for 5–10 minutes.

❺ For the dumplings, sift the flour, baking powder and salt into a bowl. Cut or rub in the butter until the mixture looks like coarse crumbs. Add the herbs. Beat together the egg yolk and milk, and stir into the flour mixture to form a soft dough, adding a little more milk, if needed.

❻ Drop the dumpling dough by rounded teaspoonfuls into the simmering soup. Cover the pan tightly and cook for 8–10 minutes, or until the dumplings are swollen and fluffy. Ladle into warmed soup plates.

# CHICKEN MINESTRONE

This chunky Mediterranean-style soup is full of goodness. You can substitute other vegetables if you wish, such as flat Italian green beans, cut in pieces, or diced celery root.

**SERVES 8–10**

| | |
|---|---|
| 150g • 5oz dried cannellini or borlotti beans, soaked overnight | 1 leek, thinly sliced |
| 4 garlic cloves, minced | 2 sage leaves, finely chopped, or ¼tsp dried |
| bouquet garni (parsley stems, thyme sprigs, rosemary sprig and bay leaf) | salt and freshly ground pepper |
| 1tbsp olive oil | 175g • 6oz sprouting broccoli, leaves cut into ribbons, stems peeled and cut in 2-cm • ¾-in pieces |
| 1 onion, finely chopped | 3 small courgettes, halved lengthwise and sliced |
| 2.5l • 4½pt chicken stock | 100g • 3½oz small pasta shapes |
| 200g • 7oz cubed cooked chicken | |
| 350g • 12oz diced pumpkin | |

❶ Drain the beans, put in a saucepan with cold water to cover and set over high heat. Bring to the boil and boil for 10 minutes. Drain, rinse and return to the pan. Add half the garlic and the bouquet garni, and cover generously with fresh water. Bring to the boil, reduce the heat to low and simmer until tender, 1–1½ hours, adding boiling water as needed to keep the beans covered by at least 2.5cm/1in. Discard the bouquet garni.

❷ Heat the oil in a large heavy saucepan over medium heat and add the onion. Cook for 2–3 minutes until slightly softened, stirring occasionally, then add the remaining garlic and continue cooking for 2 minutes, stirring frequently. Add the stock, the beans and their cooking liquid, chicken, pumpkin, leek and sage, and season to taste with salt and pepper. Bring to the boil, reduce the heat to medium-low and simmer for 5 minutes. Stir in the sprouting broccoli, courgettes and pasta, and continue cooking for 15–20 minutes longer, or until the pasta and all the vegetables are tender.

❸ Taste and adjust the seasoning, and ladle into warmed bowls.

# SMOKED CHICKEN *and* LENTIL SOUP

Lentils are often paired with ham, as smoked meats seem to give a pleasing element of richness. Smoked chicken, or other smoked poultry or game, offers a more subtle and complex combination of flavours.

**SERVES 4**

| | |
|---|---|
| 15g • ½oz butter | bouquet garni (thyme sprigs, celery leaves, sage and bay leaf) |
| 2 leeks, split and thinly sliced | |
| 2 carrots, finely chopped | |
| 1 large onion, finely chopped | 1l • 1¾pt chicken stock |
| 1 garlic clove, minced | 175g • 6oz cubed smoked chicken |
| 150g • 5oz dried lentils (preferably Puy) | salt and freshly ground pepper |
| 500ml • 18fl oz water | |

❶ Melt the butter in a large saucepan or stockpot over medium heat. Add the leeks, carrots, onion and garlic, and cook for 4–5 minutes until slightly softened, stirring frequently.

❷ Rinse and drain the lentils, and check for any small stones. Add to the vegetables with the water and bouquet garni. Bring to the boil, reduce the heat to medium-low and simmer for about 30 minutes, or until the lentils are just tender.

❸ Add the chicken, season to taste with salt and pepper, and continue cooking for 15 minutes. Remove the bouquet garni and ladle into a warmed tureen or bowls.

~.~.~.~.~.~.~.~.~.~

*TO DRINK*
An oaky Chardonnay
or a light dry red
wine.

~.~.~.~.~.~.~.~.~.~

# CHICKEN SOUP *with* HOMEMADE NOODLES

These rich golden egg noodles are worth the effort, but if time is short, save noodle-making for another day and simmer good quality bought fresh pasta in the soup. Scientific studies indicate that chicken soup, long held to be a panacea for minor ailments, does have certain restorative properties – but don't reserve this soup for illness!

**SERVES 6**

*4 chicken leg quarters, about*
  *800g • 1¾lb, skinned*
*2l • 3½pt chicken stock*
*1 celery stick, roughly chopped*
*1 carrot, roughly chopped*
*1 onion, sliced*
*1 garlic clove, crushed*
*5 peppercorns*
*large bouquet garni (parsley*
  *stems, thyme sprigs and*
  *bay leaf)*

*15g • ½oz butter*
*150g • 5oz mushrooms, sliced*
*2tbsp chopped fresh parsley*
NOODLES
*115g • 4oz strong plain flour*
*¼tsp salt*
*2 egg yolks*
*1tsp extra-virgin olive oil*
*pinch saffron threads, soaked*
  *in 2tbsp hot water*

❶ For the noodles, put the flour and salt into a food processor fitted with a steel blade and pulse to combine. In a small bowl, beat together the egg yolks and oil, strain in the saffron liquid and beat to mix; discard the threads. With the machine running, pour in the egg yolk mixture and continue running until it all comes together and forms a ball which leaves the bowl virtually clean. If this doesn't happen and the dough seems a bit sticky, add 15–30ml/1–2tbsp plain flour and continue kneading in the food processor until it forms a ball and the dough does not stick to your hands. Wrap and chill for at least 30 minutes.

❷ Divide the dough into quarters and roll out on a lightly floured surface as thinly as possible, less than 1.5mm/¹⁄₁₆in, and cut into diamond shapes about 4cm/1½in on each side. Alternatively, use a pasta machine to roll the dough into wide strips and cut them into noodles about 1cm /⅜in wide. Let the noodles dry in a single layer on floured wire racks or baking trays for about 1 hour. (If making ahead, leave to dry for about 3 hours and store in a plastic bag, refrigerated, for up to 1 day.)

❸ Put the chicken in a large saucepan with the stock, celery, carrot, onion, garlic, peppercorns and bouquet garni. Bring just to the boil over medium-high heat, skimming off the foam that rises to the surface. Reduce the heat to medium-low and simmer, partially covered, for about 45 minutes, or until the chicken is tender, skimming as needed.

❹ Remove the chicken from the stock and set aside to cool. Continue simmering the stock, uncovered, for about 30 minutes. When the chicken is cool enough to handle, take the meat from the bones and cut into bite-sized pieces. Strain the stock and remove as much fat as possible; discard the bouquet garni and vegetables.

❺ Melt the butter in a large saucepan or flameproof casserole over medium heat. Add the mushrooms and 1tbsp water and cook until lightly browned, stirring frequently. Add the stock and allow to come to the boil. Stir in the noodles and boil gently for 10 minutes, return the chicken to the stock and continue cooking for 5–10 minutes longer, or until the noodles are tender. Ladle the soup into warmed shallow bowls and sprinkle with parsley.

# PHEASANT SOUP *with* LIVER DUMPLINGS

This soup is great for gourmet hunters (and shooters)! Make it after roasting pheasant, using leftover cooked meat and stock made from the carcasses, or make stock from the remaining parts of raw birds after the breasts have been removed for serving separately.

**SERVES 4**

1.5l • 2¾pt pheasant stock
275g • 10oz cubed cooked pheasant
1tbsp chopped fresh parsley
1tbsp chopped fresh chives and/or tarragon
LIVER DUMPLINGS
15g • ½oz butter, plus more for frying
1 shallot, finely chopped
100g • 3½oz pheasant or chicken livers
1 egg, beaten
1tbsp whipping cream
75g • 2½oz fresh white breadcrumbs
1tsp chopped fresh thyme
salt and freshly ground pepper

❶ Combine the stock and pheasant meat in a saucepan. Bring to the boil, reduce the heat to low and simmer for about 15 minutes.
❷ For the liver dumplings, melt half the butter in a small frying pan over medium-low heat and cook the shallots and garlic for 3–4 minutes until softened. Remove to cool. Add the remaining butter, increase the heat to medium-high and cook the livers for 2–3 minutes until browned, turning to colour evenly. Remove and leave to cool slightly. Beat together the egg and cream in a small bowl. Add the bread-crumbs, stir to combine and leave to stand until the bread has absorbed the egg, 1–2 minutes. Put the livers in a food processor fitted with a steel blade and pulse to chop finely. Add the thyme, shallots, garlic and soaked bread, and pro-cess to mix well.
❸ To cook the dumplings, melt a little butter in a frying pan over medium heat. Shape the mixture into small balls about the size of chestnuts. Flatten them slightly and fry gently until lightly browned, about 3 minutes, turning once. Drain on paper towels.
❹ Divide the dumplings among warmed soup bowls. Ladle over the hot soup and sprinkle with herbs.

~.~.~.~.~.~.~.~.~.~

*TO DRINK*
Madeira or a fine old dry Oloroso sherry.

~·~·~·~·~·~·~·~·~·~

# CURRIED CHICKEN CHOWDER

The subtle curry and slightly tart apple flavours give this soup a pleasing complexity that makes it suitable for the most elegant occasions, but equally appealing for a cosy lunch. The strength of curry powders vary, so use your own judgment, but it should not dominate.

**SERVES 4**

25g • 1oz butter
1 onion, finely chopped
1 garlic clove, minced
25g • 1oz plain flour
1tsp curry powder
2 small carrots, halved lengthwise and thinly sliced
1 celery stick, finely sliced
1 potato, diced
1l • 1¾pt chicken stock
bouquet garni
salt and freshly ground pepper
1 dessert apple, peeled, cored and diced
225g • 8oz cubed cooked chicken
4–6tbsp whipping cream
2tbsp chopped fresh chives, to garnish

❶ Melt the butter in a large heavy saucepan over medium heat. Add the onion and garlic. Cook, stirring frequently, until the vegetables start to soften, about 5 minutes. Stir in the flour and curry powder and cook for 2 minutes. Stir in the carrots, celery, potato and stock. Bring to the boil, stirring frequently. Add the bouquet garni and season with salt and pepper.
❷ Reduce the heat to medium-low and simmer, stirring occasionally, until the vegetables are almost tender, about 20 minutes. Add the apple and chicken, and continue cooking for about 10 minutes, or until the apple is tender.
❸ Stir in the cream, taste and adjust the seasoning, and heat through. Ladle into warmed bowls and garnish with chives.

~.~.~.~.~.~.~.~.~.~

*TO DRINK*
A well-chilled dry
Fino sherry.

~·~·~·~·~·~·~·~·~·~

# CABBAGE AND BEAN SOUP
## *with* PRESERVED DUCK *or* GOOSE

Cited by Curnonsky, the renowned French gastronome, as one of the four great regional dishes, this soup from Béarn, north of the Pyrenées, has many local and seasonal variations, such as the addition of Swiss chard or kale, chestnuts or garlic sausage. It should be thick enough for a spoon to stand upright and is usually cooked in a special earthenware kettle.

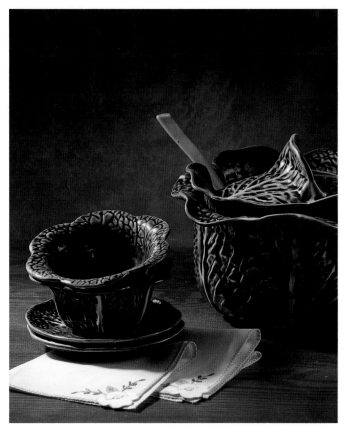

**SERVES 8–10**

*450g • 1lb dried haricot beans, soaked overnight in cold water to cover generously*
*3–4 leg pieces preserved duck or goose* (confit), *with fat*
*2 onions, finely chopped*
*450g • 1lb lean salt pork, rind removed, diced*
*2.5l • 4½pt duck or chicken stock, or water*
*225g • 8oz boneless pork shoulder*
*bouquet garni (parsley stems, thyme and marjoram sprigs, and bay leaf, tied)*
*1 onion, studded with 3–4 cloves*

*2 leeks, halved lengthwise and finely sliced*
*2 carrots, sliced*
*2 white turnips, quartered*
*4 garlic cloves, minced*
*salt and freshly ground pepper*
*1 medium green cabbage, quartered*
*3 potatoes, cubed*
*2tbsp chopped fresh parsley*
*16–20 slices of country-style French bread, for serving (optional)*
*about 115g • 4oz grated Gruyère cheese, for serving (optional)*

❶ Drain the beans, put in a saucepan with cold water to cover and set over high heat. Bring to the boil and boil for 10 minutes. Drain and add fresh cold water to cover. Bring to the boil again, drain and rinse well.

❷ Scrape the fat from the *confit* and reserve separately from the meat.

❸ Heat 3tbsp of the fat from the *confit* in a large flameproof casserole over medium-high heat. Add the chopped onions and salt pork and cook until lightly browned, stirring frequently. Add the beans, stock, pork, bouquet garni and studded onion. Simmer over low heat for 1 hour, skimming off the fat and stirring occasionally.

❹ Add the leeks, carrots, turnips and half the garlic and continue cooking for 20 minutes, or until the beans and meat are tender, stirring constantly. Taste and season with salt, if needed, and pepper.

❺ Bring a large saucepan of salted water to the boil and add the cabbage. Cook, uncovered, for 10 minutes, rinse under cold water and drain.

❻ Add the cabbage and potatoes to the beans with the cooked ham, the remaining garlic and the parsley. Stir to combine and add the pieces of confit. Continue simmering gently for 45 minutes, or until all the vegetables are tender.

❼ Preheat the oven to 200°C/400°F/Gas 6. If you wish, transfer the soup to an ovenproof tureen. Arrange the bread over the top and sprinkle lightly with grated cheese. Place on the top shelf of the oven and bake until the top is browned, about 10 minutes.

~.~.~.~.~.~.~.~.~.~

*TO DRINK*
A hearty red wine
from southwest
France.

~·~·~·~·~·~·~·~·~·~

# BRUNSWICK CHICKEN SOUP

This soup/stew, which is thought to have originated in Virginia, was traditionally served at political rallys, family reunions and other large gatherings due to its variable and expandable nature. Early versions contained small game, and rabbit or game birds would be suitable substitutes for chicken if you wish to improvise.

**SERVES 6**

*1kg • 2¼lb chicken thighs or leg quarters*
*4–5tbsp dry white wine*
*1.5l • 2¾pt chicken stock*
*2 carrots, sliced*
*large bouquet garni (parsley stems, thyme sprigs, celery leaves and bay leaf)*
*50g • 2oz butter*
*175g • 6oz button mushrooms, sliced*

*1 onion, finely chopped*
*1 garlic clove, minced*
*25g • 1oz plain flour*
*3 tomatoes, peeled, deseeded and chopped*
*175g • 6oz fresh or thawed frozen lima beans (or broad beans)*
*200g • 7oz sweetcorn kernels*
*salt and freshly ground pepper*

❶ Put the chicken pieces, skin side down, in one layer in a large deep frying pan or flameproof casserole. Set over medium-high heat and cook until the chicken is evenly browned, turning once. Pour off all the rendered fat and add the wine. Cook for 1 minute and add the stock, stirring and scraping the bottom of the pan. Add the carrots and bouquet garni. Bring just to the boil, skimming off any foam that rises to the surface. Reduce the heat to medium-low and simmer, partially covered, for 35–40 minutes until the chicken is tender, skimming from time to time.

❷ Using a slotted spoon, transfer the carrots and chicken pieces from the cooking liquid to a bowl. When the chicken is cool enough to handle, skin it and take the meat from the bones; discard the skin and bones. Cut the meat into small pieces and reserve with the carrots. Remove as much fat as possible from the cooking liquid and discard the bouquet garni.

❸ In a large saucepan or flameproof casserole, melt half the butter over medium-high heat. Add the mushrooms and cook, stirring frequently until golden. Transfer to the bowl with the carrots and chicken meat.

❹ Melt the remaining butter, add the onion and garlic, and cook, stirring frequently, over medium-low heat until just soft, about 5 minutes. Stir in the flour and cook for 2 minutes, stirring occasionally. Gradually pour in a third of the cooking liquid, whisking constantly. Bring to the boil, whisking, and cook for 2 minutes. Whisk in the remaining liquid until smooth. Add the tomatoes, lima (or broad) beans and sweetcorn with the reserved chicken and vegetables. Bring back to the boil, reduce the heat to medium-low, and simmer until the beans are tender, about 20 minutes. Taste and adjust the seasoning and ladle into warmed soup bowls.

~.~.~.~.~.~.~.~.~.~

*To Drink*
Fino Sherry

~·~·~·~·~·~·~·~·~·~

CHAPTER FOUR

# Seafood Soups

Soups capitalizing on the bounty of the sea are universal. They may be an appetite tempter or the mainstay of a meal, but when you inhale the rising steam laden with briney aromas, you can almost hear the waves breaking. Modern transportation ensures that even inland areas are blessed with a rich array of fish and shellfish – and seafood soups are as good for us as they are tasty.

# SEAFOOD SOUPS

*A*ll countries with a coastline have a tradition of seafood soups and these vary enormously. Many were developed to utilize the diverse remains of unsold fish and shellfish from the day's catch and to make them go further. There is, consequently, room for improvisation in this kind of soup.

*Fish stock is the quickest of any to make and some shellfish, such as molluscs, make their own stock. Mussels and clams release a flavourful liquid during cooking which can, and should, be used in any soup from which they are made. Even the non-edible parts of some shellfish, such as the carapace, offer the makings of a flavourful stock – so don't throw away those prawn or shrimp shells; boil them up.*

*Take care to avoid overcooking. Fish and shellfish are usually added towards the end of the cooking time of a soup, even though*

Traditionally, fish soups vary with the catch. What is available determines what goes into the soup and the contents are likely to change from one time to the next. Most of the regional classics, such as Bouillabaisse, have local variations, particular to each village where it is made.

70

some parts may have been used in the initial preparation of the stock. Reheating fish soups is tricky. If you can't avoid it, strain off all the seafood and reheat the liquid, putting back the seafood just long enough to heat through.

The soups in this chapter offer a good way to enjoy all sorts of seafood. The more substantial soups, such as Bouillabaisse or Shrimp Gumbo, are traditionally served as a main course, perhaps with bread and a salad, and the estimated number of servings reflects this. If served as a starter, they are most appropriate before a relatively simple and light main course. Others, such as Creamy Mussel Soup, are normally served as a first course. Enjoy these soups when and as you like, adjusting the proportion of liquid to seafood – either more or less – to suit.

~·~·~·~·~·~·~·~·~·~

*"This Bouillabaisse a noble dish is –*
*A sort of soup, or broth, or brew,*
*Or hotchpotch of all sorts of fishes,*
*That Greenwich never could outdo;*
*Green herbs, red peppers, mussels, saffron,*
*Soles, onions, garlic, roach, and dace;*
*All these to eat at Terré's tavern*
*In that one dish of Bouillabaisse."*

"Ballad of Bouillabaiise"
*W. M. Thackeray, 1811–63*

~·~·~·~·~·~·~·~·~·~

# PROVENCAL FISH SOUP

This rich soup, made from small rockfish and other essentially unsaleable fish, is found in virtually every restaurant along the Mediterranean coast – and it is usually wonderful. In Marseilles, pasta is added to the soup.

**SERVES 6**

*1.25kg • 2½lb small fish, gutted (use any sort except strong oily fish such as mackerel)*
*2tbsp olive oil*
*1 onion, halved and sliced*
*1 small fennel bulb, sliced*
*675g • 1½lb ripe tomatoes, cored and quartered, or scant 600ml • 1pt canned chopped Italian tomatoes in juice*
*2 garlic cloves, sliced*
*bouquet garni (thyme sprigs, parsley stems and bay leaf)*
*zest of 1 orange, removed with a vegetable peeler*
*2 pinches saffron threads, dissolved in 2tbsp boiling water*
*750ml • 1¼pt water*
*salt and freshly ground black pepper*
To Serve
*croutons (see page 122)*
*rouille (see page 124)*

❶ Wash the fish under cold running water to remove any blood. Cut each fish into three or four pieces.
❷ Heat the olive oil in a large non-reactive saucepan or flameproof casserole. Add the onion and fennel, and cook over moderate heat, stirring occasionally, for 3–4 minutes, until the onion starts to soften.
❸ Add the fish, tomatoes, garlic, bouquet garni, orange zest, saffron and water. Reduce the heat and simmer, partially covered, for 30 minutes, stirring once or twice.
❹ Discard the bouquet garni and purée the fish and vegetable mixture in a food processor fitted with a steel blade, then work the mixture through the medium blade of a food mill or press through a sturdy sieve into the saucepan.
❺ Set the saucepan over medium heat, taste and adjust the seasoning, and simmer until the soup is heated through.

~.~.~.~.~.~.~.~.~.~

*VARIATION*
Add 50g/2oz broken
spaghetti or other small
pasta, cooked in boiling
salted water until tender,
after the soup has
been puréed.

~.~.~.~.~.~.~.~.~.~

# CURRIED CRAB SOUP

Serve with croutons and *rouille*, if you wish. Female crabs are best for soup because the roe adds flavour and colour. This recipe, also known as She-crab Soup, is traditional in the American South.

**SERVES 4–6**

*65g • 2½oz butter*
*1 shallot, finely chopped*
*4tbsp plain flour*
*½tsp curry powder*
*2–3tbsp sherry*
*150ml • ¼pt shellfish stock or bottled clam juice diluted with water*
*bay leaf*
*575g • 1¼lb tomatoes, peeled, deseeded and chopped*
*250ml • 8fl oz single cream*
*225g • 8oz crab meat, picked over*
*salt and freshly ground black pepper*
*Tabasco sauce (optional)*
*4–6 crab claws, cracked and peeled, to garnish*

❶ Melt the butter in a saucepan over medium-low heat. Add the shallot and cook for about 5 minutes until softened, stirring frequently. Stir in the flour and curry powder, and cook for 2 minutes. Add the sherry and cook, stirring constantly, until smooth and thick.
❷ Gradually stir in the stock and add the bay leaf and tomatoes. Simmer, stirring occasionally, for about 15 minutes, until the vegetables are soft.
❸ Work the soup through the medium blade of a food mill set over a bowl. (The soup may be prepared in advance up to this point. Leave to cool, cover and chill. Reheat gently over low heat before continuing.)
❹ Stir in the cream and crab meat. Taste and adjust the seasoning, and add a few drops of Tabasco sauce, if you wish. Ladle into warmed bowls or a tureen and garnish with crab claws.

~.~.~.~.~.~.~.~.~.~

*TO DRINK*
A fruity, slightly
spicy medium-dry
white, such as
Gewürztraminer.

~.~.~.~.~.~.~.~.~.~

# OYSTERS IN PARSLEY *and* GARLIC CREAM

The parsley in this creamy soup tames the garlic and gives it a brilliant colour. It is delicious made with plump succulent oysters, but if you prefer, you can substitute mussels or cooked snails.

**SERVES 4**

16–20 oysters

1 large bunch of curly parsley, stems removed (about 115g • 4oz leaves)

350ml • 12fl oz whipping cream

1–2 garlic cloves, finely chopped

3–4tbsp shellfish stock or water (optional)

salt and freshly ground pepper

1 ripe tomato (preferably plum), peeled, deseeded and diced

❶ Working over a bowl to catch the juices, open the oysters: hold in a cloth (flat-side up), push the knife into the hinge, then work it around until you can pry off the top shell. When all the oysters have been opened, strain the liquid through a sieve lined with damp muslin. Remove the oysters from their shells and rinse under cold running water removing any bits of shell that adhere. Return the oysters to the filtered liquid. (This may be done several hours in advance; chill, covered.)

❷ Bring a large saucepan of salted water to the boil. Drop in the parsley leaves and cook for 3–4 minutes until bright green and tender. Drain and refresh in cold water. Press with the back of a spoon to extract as much water as possible. (This may be done up to 1 day in advance; chill.)

❸ Combine the cream and garlic in a medium saucepan and simmer over medium-low heat for 15 minutes until the garlic is tender and the cream has thickened slightly. Transfer to a blender or a food processor fitted with a steel blade, add the parsley and purée until smooth. Return the purée to the saucepan and stir in the oyster liquid. If you wish, thin with shellfish stock or water.

❹ Season to taste with salt, if needed, and pepper. Simmer the soup gently for about 5 minutes. Add the oysters and continue cooking for 1–2 minutes until the oysters are just heated through. Remove them with a slotted spoon and divide between four warmed shallow soup plates. Ladle over the soup and garnish with diced tomato.

~.~.~.~.~.~.~.~.~.~

*TO DRINK*
A dry, slightly sharp white, such as Entre-Deux-Mers, Muscadet or a North American Semillon.

~.~.~.~.~.~.~.~.~.~

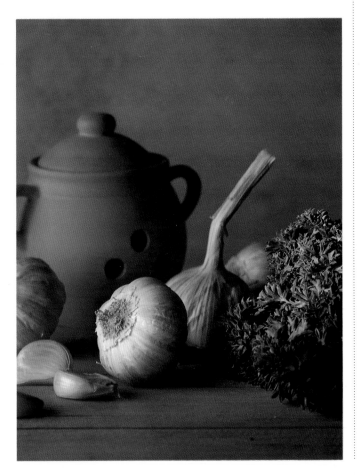

# ITALIAN FISH SOUP

*(Brodetto)*

Like bouillabaisse, its counterpart in France, *brodetto* has innumerable variations. What distinguishes *brodetto* is braising the onions in vinegar for the soup base. Folklore dictates that 13 kinds of fish should be included, but unless you are feeding a crowd, this may not be practical. Use several kinds of firm white-fleshed fish and avoid particularly oily ones. According to tradition, the fish should not be too "noble" – this is the food of fishermen.

**SERVES 6–8**

*2tbsp extra-virgin olive oil*
*2 onions, chopped*
*5tbsp white wine vinegar*
*2 garlic cloves, very finely chopped*
*1 carrot, grated*
*450g • 1lb ripe tomatoes, peeled, deseeded and chopped, or 400ml • 14fl oz canned chopped Italian tomatoes in juice*
*475ml • 16fl oz dry white wine*
*1–2tbsp tomato purée*
*350ml • 12fl oz fish stock, or 250ml • 8fl oz water*

*225g • 8oz squid, cleaned, skinned and cut into rings*
*grated zest of 1 lemon*
*bay leaf*
*1kg • 2¼lb white fish fillets, such as red snapper, cod, haddock, monkfish, shark or swordfish, skinned if wished and cut into pieces*
*450g • 1lb small clams, scrubbed*
*chopped fresh parsley, to garnish*
*large garlic croutons (see page 122), to serve*

❶ Heat the oil in a heavy non-reactive saucepan or flameproof casserole over medium heat. Add the onions and cook until softened, about 3 minutes. Add the vinegar and cook, stirring frequently, until the vinegar has evaporated and continue cooking until the onions are golden.

❷ Add the garlic and carrot to the onion mixture, cook for 2–3 minutes and stir in the tomatoes and wine. Bring to the boil and boil for 1 minute. Stir in the tomato purée, stock or water and the squid, lemon zest and bay leaf. Reduce the heat to low and simmer, partially covered, until the squid is tender, about 30 minutes, stirring occasionally.

❸ Arrange the thicker pieces of fish over the mixture and push them into the soup. Put the thinner pieces of fish and the clams over the top, cover and continue simmering for about 5 minutes longer, or until the fish is opaque throughout and the clams have opened. Ladle into a warmed tureen or bowls, sprinkle with parsley and serve with garlic croutons.

~.~.~.~.~.~.~.~.~.~

*COOK'S TIP*
The soup may be prepared several hours in advance except for adding the fish and shellfish. Leave to cool, cover and chill. Reheat to simmering before continuing with step 3. If you wish, omit the squid and clams, and use only white fish, increasing the amount to about 1.25kg/2½lb.

*TO DRINK*
A crisp white country wine, such as Verdicchio or Frascati.

~·~·~·~·~·~·~·~·~

# BLACK *and* WHITE
# SQUID SOUP

This soup has a spare, almost Oriental look, but the flavours are more Mediterranean. Black squid ink pasta is found in specialist shops featuring Italian gourmet products or in food halls of department stores. It doesn't taste particularly "fishy", so if you wish, substitute other small coloured pasta shapes.

**SERVES 4**

*350g • 12oz squid, cleaned, skinned and cut into thin rings*
*juice of 1 lemon*
*75g • 3oz squid ink pasta*

*900ml • 1½pt fish or shellfish stock*
*pinch of saffron threads, soaked in 3tbsp boiling water*
*salt and white pepper*

❶ Put the squid in a non-reactive saucepan with the lemon juice and water to cover generously. Bring to the boil, reduce the heat to low and simmer, partially covered, until the squid is tender, up to 1½ hours, adding more water if needed.

❷ Bring a moderately large saucepan of salted water to the boil, add the pasta and cook until tender but still a little chewy, *al dente*. Drain and rinse under cold running water.

❸ Bring the stock to the boil, strain in the saffron water and season with salt if needed and pepper to taste. Add the squid and pasta, and simmer for about 5 minutes until heated through. Ladle into a warmed tureen or bowl.

~.~.~.~.~.~.~.~.~.~

*COOK'S TIP*
To clean squid, hold the sac-like body gently in one hand and the head in the other. Pull the head away from the body: the entrails should come with it. Rinse the sac under cold running water, loosen the transparent "bone" and pull it out. Gently squeeze out any remaining material inside the body and rinse again. Slice off the fins and slice the body into rings. Cut off and discard the part of the head above the tentacles containing the eyes and remove any hard central part. Ready-cooked squid rings are sometimes available in fishmongers and supermarkets, and will save the time spent preparing and cooking the squid.

~·~·~·~·~·~·~·~·~·~

# CREAMY MUSSEL SOUP

Variations of this soup are found all over France. This un-adulterated version focuses on the briny flavour of the mussels. Sometimes saffron is added, as in Billi-Bi, the soup made famous at Maxime's in Paris, or other spices, such as the curry that is typical in Brittany.

**SERVES 4**

2kg • 4½lb mussels
150ml • ¼pt dry white wine
bouquet garni (thyme sprigs, parsley stems and bay leaf)
freshly ground pepper
15g • ½oz butter

2 large shallots, finely chopped
1 carrot, finely diced
300ml • ½pt whipping cream
1tbsp cornflour, dissolved in 2tbsp water
2tbsp chopped fresh parsley

❶ Discard any broken mussels and those with open shells that refuse to close when tapped. Under cold running water, scrape the mussel shells with a knife to remove any barnacles and pull out the stringy "beards". Rinse in several changes of cold water.

❷ In a large heavy saucepan or flameproof casserole combine the wine, bouquet garni and plenty of pepper. Bring to the boil over medium-high heat and cook for 2 minutes. Add the mussels, cover tightly and cook for about 5 minutes, or until the mussels open, shaking the pan occasionally.

❸ When they are cool enough to handle, remove the mussels from the shells, straining any additional juices into the cooking liquid. Strain the cooking liquid through a muslin-lined sieve.

❹ Melt the butter in a heavy saucepan. Add the shallots and carrot, and cook until the shallots are soft, stirring occasionally. Stir in the mussel cooking liquid and bring to the boil. Reduce the heat to low and simmer until the vegetables are tender, about 30 minutes.

❺ Add the cream and bring just to the boil. Stir the dissolved cornflour and stir it into the soup. Boil gently for 2–3 minutes until slightly thickened, stirring frequently. Add the mussels and cook for about 1–2 minutes longer to reheat them. Stir in the parsley and ladle into a warmed tureen or soup bowls.

# SMOKED SALMON CHOWDER

This rich, thick soup is full of flavour – a heartwarming lunch on a chilly day or an elegant, if substantial, starter. The poached salmon keeps it from being too salty and makes a tasty broth.

**SERVES 6**

15g • ½oz butter
3–4 shallots, finely chopped
2 celery sticks, finely chopped
1.2l • 2pt water
1 bay leaf
2 salmon steaks, about 450g/1lb total weight

2 potatoes, about 450g • 1lb, diced
300ml • ½pt single cream
freshly ground black pepper
200g • 7oz smoked salmon, cut in bite-sized pieces
1tbsp chopped fresh dill
1tbsp chopped fresh chives

❶ Melt the butter in a heavy non-reactive saucepan over medium-low heat. Add the shallots and celery, and sweat until slightly softened. Add the water and bay leaf, cover and simmer for 10 minutes.

❷ Add the salmon steaks and poach for 10 minutes over low heat, covered. Transfer with a fish slice to a plate and leave to cool slightly. Discard the salmon skin and bones, and flake the flesh coarsely.

❸ Meanwhile, stir the potatoes into the cooking liquid and continue simmering for 15–20 minutes, partially covered, until they are tender.

❹ Add the cream to the chowder, season with pepper and simmer for about 5 minutes to heat through. Stir in the poached salmon, smoked salmon pieces and herbs, and continue cooking for 5 minutes. Taste and adjust the seasoning, and ladle into warmed soup plates or bowls.

~.~.~.~.~.~.~.~.~.~

*TO DRINK*
A rich, lightly oaked
Chardonnay, or
perhaps a dry
Amontillado sherry.

~.~.~.~.~.~.~.~.~.~

# SHELLFISH BISQUE

In Cajun cuisine, crayfish are typically used to make this soup, but virtually any kind of shellfish is suitable – small prawns, scampi, crabs or lobsters. Use a mixture if you wish – most of the flavour comes from the shells, so you could even make this soup after you have eaten the lobster!

**SERVES 4**

*350g • 12oz small cooked*
  *prawns in the shell, or 450g*
  *• 1lb with heads if possible,*
  *or about 675g • 1½lb hard-*
  *shelled shellfish, such as*
  *crabs, scampi or lobster*
*25g • 1oz butter*
*25g • 1oz plain flour*
*2tbsp Cognac*
*cayenne pepper*
*4–5tbsp whipping cream*
*lemon juice*

STOCK
*2tsp vegetable oil*
*shellfish shells and heads, or*
  *chopped small shellfish (at*
  *least 250–450g • 8oz–1lb)*
*1 onion, halved and sliced*
*1 small carrot, sliced*
*1 celery stick, sliced*
*1l • 1¾pt water*
*½ lemon, sliced*
*bouquet garni (thyme sprigs,*
  *parsley stems and bay leaf)*

~·~·~·~·~·~·~·~·~·~

*COOK'S TIP*
If you have bought raw shellfish,
cook it in boiling water and use
the cooking water for the stock.
If using tiny crabs, the task of
extracting any meat is too arduous,
but chop them and cook
as for shells.

~·~·~·~·~·~·~·~·~

❶ Remove the shells and heads, if any, from the shellfish, reserving them for the stock. For crab, scampi or lobster, chop the shells in small pieces. Cover and chill the shellfish meat, either for use in the soup or for another purpose.

❷ For the stock, heat the oil in a large saucepan over high heat. Add the shellfish shells and heads, if any, and sauté until they start to brown. Reduce the heat to medium and add the onion, carrot and celery. Cook, stirring occasionally, for about 5 minutes, until the onion starts to soften. Add the water, lemon and bouquet garni. Bring to the boil, reduce the heat to low and simmer gently, partially covered, for 25 minutes. Strain the stock.

❸ Melt the butter in a heavy saucepan over moderate heat. Stir in the flour and cook until slightly golden, stirring occasionally. Add the Cognac and gradually pour in about half the stock, whisking vigorously until smooth, then add the remaining stock, still whisking. Season with cayenne pepper (salt is not usually needed). Reduce the heat, cover and simmer gently for about 5 minutes, stirring occasionally.

❹ Strain the soup if not completely smooth. Add the cream and lemon juice to taste. Reheat the shellfish meat, if using, briefly in the soup before serving.

~·~·~·~·~·~·~·~·~·~

*TO DRINK*
A rich, fruity dry
white wine, such as
Pinot Gris or
Chardonnay, or dry
fino sherry.

~·~·~·~·~·~·~·~·~

# BRITTANY SEAFOOD SOUP

*(Cotriade)*

This creamy, French-style chowder is full of fish and shell-fish from the northern coastal waters. The sorrel gives it a pleasant piquancy, but if it is difficult to find, just omit it and add a squeeze of lemon juice. Alternatively, stir a tea-spoonful of curry powder into the cream before adding – Breton ports played an important role in the spice trade and such spices are not unusual in the regional cuisine.

**SERVES 8**

*1kg • 2¼lb mussels, scrubbed
and de-bearded*
*90ml • 3fl oz dry cider or
white wine*
*freshly ground black pepper*
*25g • 1oz butter*
*2 leeks, thinly sliced*
*1 large onion, finely chopped*
*450g • 1lb potatoes, diced*
*1.2l • 2pt fish stock*
*bouquet garni (thyme sprigs,
parsley stems and bay leaf)*
*150g • 5oz fresh sorrel leaves,*

*washed and blotted dry*
*675g • 1½lb white fish fillets,
such as cod, turbot and
monkfish, skinned and cut
into large bite-sized pieces*
*350g • 12oz cooked or raw
medium prawns or crayfish,
peeled*
*350g • 12oz small scallops*
*250ml • 8fl oz double cream or
crème fraîche*
*large croutons, to serve
(optional)*

❶ Put the mussels into a large heavy saucepan with the cider or wine and a little pepper. Steam, tightly covered, over high heat until the shells open (discard any that refuse to open). When cool enough to handle, remove the mussels from the shells. Strain and reserve the cooking liquid.

❷ Melt half the butter in a wide flameproof casserole or sauté pan over medium-low heat. Cook the leeks and onion until the onion starts to soften, about 3 minutes. Stir in the potatoes, stock and the strained mussel cooking juices. Bring to the boil, add the bouquet garni and reduce the heat to medium-low. Simmer, partially covered, until the potatoes are just tender, about 20 minutes.

❸ Melt the remaining butter in a small frying pan or saucepan over low heat. Add the sorrel until it is wilted and remove from the heat.

❹ Add the fish to the soup, starting with the thickest pieces and putting in the thinner ones after 1–2 minutes. A few minutes after all the fish has been added, add the prawns, scallops and mussels, and continue simmering gently for 2–3 minutes until all the seafood is cooked (the flesh is opaque throughout). Using a slotted spoon, transfer the fish and shellfish to a warmed tureen and cover to keep warm.

❺ Bring the soup to the boil and stir in the cream and the sorrel. Continue boiling gently, stirring occasionally, for 4–5 minutes until slightly reduced and thickened. Taste for seasoning and ladle the soup over the fish and shellfish. Serve with croutons, if you wish.

# CLAM CHILLI

Clams are often underrated, but they are wonderfully versatile. This "chilli" is thick and spicy, and the meaty texture of the clams gives it body and brings an aromatic marine element that makes it quite exotic.

**SERVES 6–8**

*200g • 7oz dried black beans or haricot beans, soaked overnight in cold water to cover generously, or 1 400-g • 14-oz can black or cannellini beans, rinsed*
*120ml • 4fl oz dry white wine*
*1.75kg • 4lb small or medium-sized clams, scrubbed, or 2 275-g • 10-oz cans baby clams, drained, plus 350ml • 12 fl oz bottled clam juice*
*2tbsp olive oil*
*2 onions, finely chopped*
*1 large carrot, finely chopped*
*1 celery stick, finely chopped*
*1 small red or yellow pepper, deseeded and finely chopped*
*3–4 garlic cloves, minced*
*1–2 roasted ancho or jalapeño chillies, finely chopped*
*115g • 4oz chorizo or pepperoni, finely diced*
*675g • 1½lb tomatoes, peeled, seeded and chopped, or 1 400-g • 14-oz can chopped Italian tomatoes in juice*
*350ml • 12fl oz tomato juice or tomato-clam juice*
*2tbsp tomato purée*
*2tsp chilli powder, or to taste*
*bay leaf*
*¼tsp each dried thyme and oregano*
*3–4tbsp finely chopped coriander or parsley*

❶ If using dried beans, drain them, put into a saucepan with cold water to cover and set over high heat. Bring to the boil and boil for 10 minutes. Drain and add fresh cold water to cover. Bring to the boil again, reduce the heat to low and simmer until the beans are tender, 1½–2 hours.

❷ In a large heavy saucepan or flameproof casserole combine the clams and wine. Cover tightly, set over medium-high heat and cook for 2–4 minutes, or until they open, shaking the pan occasionally.

❸ Heat the oil in a large heavy saucepan or flameproof casserole over medium heat. Add the onions and cook for 5 minutes, stirring frequently. Add the carrot, celery and pepper, cover and continue cooking until the vegetables are tender, abut 3 minutes more, stirring occasionally. Stir in the garlic, chillies, chorizo or pepperoni, tomatoes, tomato juice and clam cooking liquid, or if using canned clams, add the wine and bottle clam juice, and bring to the boil.

❹ Drain the beans, reserving the cooking liquid if using dried beans. Add the beans to the soup, reduce the heat to low and simmer very gently, stirring occasionally, until the vegetables are tender and the soup is thick, about 45 minutes. If you like a thinner soup, add as much of the bean cooking liquid or water as you wish.

❺ Taste and adjust the seasoning. Stir in the clams and heat through. Ladle into a warmed tureen or bowls and sprinkle with coriander or parsley.

# PRAWN GUMBO

Gumbo is a Cajun creation with almost infinite variations. Many but not all versions contain okra, the vegetable that gives this soup its name, and the soup may be seasoned with *filé*, made from ground sassafras leaves. Most versions start with a brown roux, one of the hallmarks of Cajun cooking. Feel free to make substitutions – the Acadians, or Cajuns, as they became known, have long been recognized for their inventive use of available ingredients.

**SERVES 6–8**

*30ml • 2tbsp olive oil*
*450g • 1lb spicy sausage, cut into 2-cm • ¾-in pieces*
*75g • 3oz smoked country ham or prosciutto, diced*
*4tbsp plain flour*
*2 onions, finely chopped*
*1 small green pepper, deseeded and finely chopped*
*2 celery sticks, finely chopped*
*3–4 garlic cloves, very finely chopped*
*3–4 spring onions, finely chopped*

*575g • 1¼lb tomatoes, peeled, deseeded and chopped*
*475ml • 16fl oz water*
*bay leaf*
*¼tsp gumbo* filé *(optional)*
*450g • 1lb okra, trimmed and cut into 2-cm • ¾-in pieces*
*475–750ml • 16–24fl oz shellfish or chicken stock, or more water*
*450g • 1lb cooked shelled medium king prawns, deveined*
*hot cooked rice, to serve*

❶ Heat the oil in a Dutch oven or heavy flameproof casserole over a medium heat. Add the sausage and cook until lightly browned, then add the ham or prosciutto and continue cooking until both are browned. Remove with a slotted spoon and drain on paper towels.

❷ Pour out all but 2tbsp of the fat in the pan and sprinkle over the flour. Stir constantly until it darkens to a medium brown, about the colour of peanut butter. Stir in the onion and pepper, and cook for 2–3 minutes until they start to soften. Add the celery, garlic and spring onions, and continue cooking for 2 minutes longer, stirring occasionally.

❸ Stir in the tomatoes and water. Bring to the boil and add the bay leaf and gumbo *filé*, if using, and the sausage and ham. Reduce the heat to medium-low and simmer for 30 minutes.

❹ Bring a large saucepan of salted water to the boil, add the okra and boil for 4 minutes. Refresh in cold running water and drain well.

❺ Add the okra to the soup with 475ml/16fl oz stock or water and simmer for 15–20 minutes until the okra is tender, stirring occasionally. Thin with more stock or water, if you wish, bring to a simmer and add the prawns. Simmer until heated through, about 5 minutes. Transfer to a warmed tureen and serve with rice, or put a little rice in the bottom of warmed bowls and ladle over the gumbo.

~·~·~·~·~·~·~·~·~

*COOK'S TIP*
For maximum
flavour, buy prawns
in the shell, peel and
devein them, and
make shellfish stock
with the shells.

~·~·~·~·~·~·~·~·~

~·~·~·~·~·~·~·~·~

*TO DRINK*
A robust, spicy
red wine.

~·~·~·~·~·~·~·~·~

# MEDITERRANEAN FISH SOUP

## *(Bouillabaisse)*

All along the Mediterranean coast, from Italy to Spain, variations of this soup abound. Almost any combination of fish and shellfish can be used, as this kind of soup was originally made from anything the fishermen had left from their catch, but strong-flavoured oily fish are best avoided. A flavourful fish stock is essential, so ask the fishmonger for the heads, tails and trimmings from the fish fillets, plus extra if available.

**SERVES 8**

*1.5kg • 3lb firm white fish fillets, such as sea bass, snapper and monkfish*
*3tbsp extra-virgin olive oil*
*grated zest of 1 unwaxed or scrubbed orange*
*1 garlic clove, very finely chopped*
*pinch saffron threads*
*2tbsp Pernod (anise liquor)*
*675g • 1½lb king prawns*
*1 small fennel bulb, finely chopped*
*1 large onion, finely chopped*
*225g • 8oz small new potatoes, sliced*
*350g • 12oz sea scallops, rinsed*

TO SERVE
*croutons (see page 122)*
*rouille (see page 124)*
STOCK
*900g–1.5kg • 2–3lb fish heads, bones and trimmings*
*2tbsp olive oil*
*2 leeks, sliced*
*1 onion, halved and sliced*
*1 red pepper, cored and sliced*
*675g • 1½lb ripe tomatoes, cored and quartered*
*4 garlic cloves, sliced*
*bouquet garni (thyme sprigs, parsley stems and bay leaf)*
*zest of 1 unwaxed or scrubbed orange, removed with a vegetable peeler*
*2–3 pinches saffron threads*
*2l • 3½pt water*

❶ Cut the fish fillets in small serving pieces. Trim off any thin ragged bits and reserve for the stock. Put the fish in a bowl with 2tbsp of olive oil, the orange zest, garlic, saffron and Pernod. Turn to coat well. Peel the prawns and reserve the shells. Cover and chill the prawns and the fish separately.

❷ For the stock, rinse the fish heads, bones and trimmings under cold running water to remove any blood. Heat the olive oil in a large non-reactive saucepan or flameproof casserole. Add the leeks, onion and pepper, and cook over moderate heat, stirring occasionally, until the onion starts to soften, about 5 minutes. Add the reserved prawn shells, fish heads, bones and trimmings, and continue cooking for 2 minutes. Stir in the tomatoes, garlic, bouquet garni, orange zest, saffron and water (top up if necessary to cover ingredients). Bring to the boil, skimming off the foam as it rises, then reduce the heat and simmer, covered, for 30 minutes, skimming once or twice. Strain the stock.

❸ To finish the bouillabaisse, heat the remaining 1tbsp of olive oil in a deep sauté pan or wide flameproof casserole over medium heat. Cook the chopped fennel and onion until the onion starts to soften, about 5 minutes, then add the strained stock. Bring to the boil, add the potatoes and cook for 5 minutes. Reduce the heat to medium-low and add the fish, starting with the thickest pieces and putting in the thinner ones after 2–3 minutes. Add the prawns and scallops, and continue simmering gently until all the seafood is cooked (opaque throughout). Transfer the fish, shellfish and potatoes to a warmed tureen or soup plates. Taste for seasoning and ladle the soup over. Serve the bouillabaisse hot with croutons spread with *rouille*.

~.~.~.~.~.~.~.~.~

*COOK'S TIP*
You can prepare the *rouille* and croutons in advance and make the stock for the soup early in the day while the fish fillets marinate. Then the final assembly isn't too difficult.

~.~.~.~.~.~.~.~.~

~.~.~.~.~.~.~.~.~

*TO DRINK*
A Côtes de Provence white or rosé or white Cassis.

~.~.~.~.~.~.~.~.~

# MUSSEL *and* NEW POTATO SOUP

This light but satisfying, unusual mussel soup is full of contrasting colours and complementary flavours. It is inspired by a dish created by a Michelin-starred chef in Burgundy.

**SERVES 4–6**

2kg • 4½lb mussels
1l • 1¾pt water
8–10 garlic cloves, unpeeled (about ½ large head)
3 thyme sprigs, or ¼tsp dried thyme
3 marjoram sprigs, or ¼tsp dried marjoram
bay leaf
pinch of saffron

275g • 10oz long thin waxy potatoes, peeled and thinly sliced
2 plum tomatoes, peeled, deseeded and finely diced
large handful of spinach leaves, about 25g • 1oz, cut in thin ribbons
aïoli, to serve (see page 84)

❶ Discard any broken mussels and those with open shells that refuse to close when tapped. Under cold running water, scrape the mussel shells with a knife to remove any barnacles and pull out the stringy "beards". Rinse in several changes of cold water.
❷ Put the mussels in a large heavy saucepan or flameproof casserole and cook, tightly covered, over high heat for 4–6 minutes until the shells open, shaking the pan occasionally. When cool enough to handle, remove the mussels from the shells. Strain the cooking liquid through a muslin-lined sieve and reserve.
❸ Combine the water, garlic, thyme, marjoram, bay leaf and saffron in a saucepan. Bring to the boil over high heat, reduce the heat to medium and simmer, partially covered, for 30 minutes.
❹ Strain the herb and garlic infusion, and combine with the mussel cooking liquid. Add the potatoes and set over medium-low heat. Bring to a simmer and cook until the potatoes are tender, about 15 minutes. Add the tomatoes, spinach and mussels, and cook until the mussels are heated through. Ladle into a warmed tureen or individual bowls and serve with *aïoli*, if you wish.

# ORIENTAL SCALLOP SOUP

This exotic soup is quick and easy to prepare. Miso, used as a base for many different soups in Japan, is made from soya beans blended with other ingredients, such as barley (*mugi miso*), brown rice (*genmai miso*) or sweet rice (*shiro miso*), and fermented to develop a unique flavour. Miso made purely from soya beans (*hatcho miso*) has a stronger taste.

**SERVES 4**

1l • 1¾pt water
4tsp miso (bean paste, available at health food shops)
75g • 3oz shiitake mushrooms, stems removed
1 garlic clove, halved
2.5-cm • 1-in piece lemon grass or peeled fresh root ginger

3–4 spring onions, cut in julienne strips about 5cm • 2in long
1tsp light soy sauce, or to taste
1tsp lemon juice, or to taste
6 large sea scallops, about 225g • 8oz
coriander leaves, to garnish

❶ Bring the water to the boil in a medium saucepan. Thin the miso with a little of the water, reduce the heat to low and stir in the diluted miso.
❷ Slice the mushrooms thinly and add to the miso broth with the garlic and lemon grass or ginger. Simmer gently for 10–12 minutes, or until the mushrooms are tender. Remove the garlic and lemon grass or ginger root, and stir in the spring onion strips. Season with soy sauce and lemon juice.
❸ Pull off the coral, if any, carefully. Discard the small hard muscle on the side and slice the scallops crosswise to form two or three thinner rounds from each. Simmer the scallops and corals in the broth until the flesh becomes opaque, 1–2 minutes.
❹ Divide the scallop rounds between four warmed bowls (white if possible), ladle the soup over and float a few coriander leaves on each serving.

~.~.~.~.~.~.~.~.~.~

*COOK'S TIP*
If you like a more
fishy flavour, stir in a
small amount of
Oriental fish sauce or
anchovy paste before
serving.

~˙~˙~˙~˙~˙~˙~˙~˙~˙~

# GARLIC FISH SOUP

## *(Bourride)*

Although many of the ingredients are the same, this soup looks nothing like its "cousin" bouillabaisse and, in fact, fishmongers in the Mediterranean region sell different fish for these two soups. Smooth and white, bourride gets its creamy texture and powerful flavour from *aïoli*, a pungent garlic mayonnaise much used in Provence, which, combined with egg yolks, is used to thicken the soup. The fish is sometimes served apart from the soup. If you prefer, omit the egg yolks to thicken the soup and just stir the remaining half of the *aïoli* into the soup until combined for an equally tasty but thinner soup.

**SERVES 6**

*1.2l • 2pt fish stock or water*
*120ml • 4fl oz dry white wine*
*1 onion, chopped*
*1 leek sliced*
*zest of ½ unwaxed or scrubbed orange, removed with a vegetable peeler*
*generous pinch of fennel seeds*
*2tsp tomato purée*
*large bouquet garni (thyme sprigs, parsley stems, leek greens and bay leaf)*
*1.25kg • 2½lb firm white fish fillets or steaks, such as monkfish or turbot*
*3 egg yolks*

*2tbsp crème fraîche or double cream*
*salt and freshly ground white pepper*
*croutons, to garnish (see page 122)*
AïOLI
*3–4 garlic cloves, very finely chopped*
*1 egg yolk, at room temperature*
*salt*
*200ml • 6½fl oz extra-virgin olive oil, at room temperature*
*juice of 1 large lemon*

❶ For the *aïoli*, combine the garlic, egg yolk and a pinch of salt in a food processor fitted with a steel blade and process for 1 minute. Add the oil by drops until the mixture begins to thicken, then add the remaining oil in a thin stream. Add the lemon juice and pulse to combine. Remove about half of the *aïoli* and reserve for serving; leave the remainder in the container. (Alternatively, chill, covered, if making in advance.)

❷ Combine the stock, wine, onion, leek, orange zest, fennel seeds and tomato purée in a large saucepan or flame-proof casserole. Bring to the boil, reduce the heat to medium-low and simmer for 10 minutes. Add the fish, starting with the thickest pieces and putting in the thinner ones after 1–2 minutes. Continue simmering gently for about 5 minutes until all the fish is cooked (the flesh is opaque throughout). Using a slotted spoon, transfer the fish to a heated tureen and cover to keep warm. Strain the cooking liquid, rinse the saucepan and return the liquid to it.

❸ Add the egg yolks to the *aïoli* in the food processor and pulse to combine. Pour in 2–3 ladlefuls of the cooking liquid and process until combined. Pour back into the saucepan, add the crème fraîche or cream and stir constantly over low heat until the mixture thickens slightly, about 5 minutes. (Do not allow it to boil.) Taste and adjust the seasoning, adding salt, if needed, and white pepper. Ladle over the fish, serve with croutons and the remaining *aïoli*, if you like.

~.~.~.~.~.~.~.~.~.~

*TO DRINK*
A robust white wine
from the region, such
as Côtes du Lubéron.

~.~.~.~.~.~.~.~.~.~

# CIOPPINO

This soup, associated with San Francisco's North Beach area, is most probably derived from the Italian seafood soup, *ciuppin*. As with most seafood soups, the ingredients can be varied. This version, which uses only shellfish, calls for mussels, squid and prawns, but clams, scallops, crab claws or small lobsters may be added or substituted. Be sure to include either mussels or clams for their flavourful liquid.

**SERVES 4–6**

*450g • 1lb mussels (in the shell), scrubbed and debearded*
*1tbsp olive oil*
*1 large onion, finely chopped*
*½ fennel bulb, finely chopped*
*675g • 1½lb tomatoes, peeled, deseeded and chopped*
*2 garlic cloves, very finely chopped*

*300ml • ½pt dry white wine*
*250ml • 8fl oz tomato juice*
*120ml • 4fl oz water*
*225g • 8oz cleaned squid, cut in thin rings, boiled until tender*
*bay leaf*
*350g • 12oz cooked shelled medium prawns, deveined*
*3tbsp chopped fresh parsley*

❶ Put the mussels into a large heavy saucepan or flame-proof casserole and cook, tightly covered, over high heat for 4–6 minutes until the shells open, shaking the pan occasionally. Remove the mussels and discard any that refuse to open. Strain the cooking liquid through a muslin-lined sieve and reserve. When the mussels are cool enough to handle, set aside a few in the shells for garnishing, one or two per serving. Remove the remainder of the mussels from the shells and strain any additional juices into the cooking liquid.

❷ Heat the olive oil in a heavy saucepan over medium-low heat. Add the onion and fennel, and cook for 2–3 minutes, until just softened, stirring occasionally. Stir in the tomatoes and garlic, and continue cooking for 10 minutes. Add the wine and bring to the boil, then add the tomato juice, water, reserved mussel cooking liquid, squid and bay leaf. Reduce the heat to low and simmer until the vegetables and squid are tender, about 20 minutes.

❸ Stir in the prawns and shelled mussels, and simmer over medium-low until heated through. Remove the bay leaf, ladle into a warmed tureen or bowls and sprinkle with parsley. Garnish with the reserved whole mussels.

~.~.~.~.~.~.~.~.~.~

*TO DRINK*
A very dry white,
such as a Californian
Fumé Blanc.

~.~.~.~.~.~.~.~.~.~

CHAPTER FIVE

# Fruit Soups

Fruit is one of the jewels of the table and its versatility merits experimentation. Fruit soups provide the perfect opportunity. They may be cooling or stimulating, rich or ethereal, unctuous in texture or chunky. They may be served to begin a meal or to end it – either way, they make it memorable. This selection of fruit soups can open the door to a colourful world of creativity.

# FRUIT SOUPS

*We often think of soups as essentially savoury, but a dessert soup or a semi-sweet soup served as a first course, can hold great appeal. Fruit soups are satisfying in many ways. They are unusual and perfect to start or follow a substantial main course.*

*On a warm day, why not begin a meal with Minted Melon Soup, to revive flagging appetites with its cooling effect? Or serve a wine-based fruit soup, such as California Iced Fruit Soup – a prelude as refreshing as a fruit punch – and much more memorable.*

*Fruit soup is often uncooked to retain the natural flavours. In its simplest form, it consists of puréed fruit combined with some other ingredient to enhance its flavour. The fruit may need to be heated briefly to make it juicier. These uncooked fruit soups should*

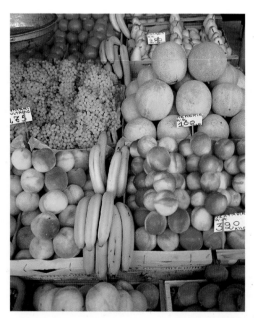

*be consumed within a day. Those that contain cooked ingredients keep longer. Most fruit soups are not thickened in the way that savoury soups might be, and flour or starch is almost never used. If puréed, the fruit itself becomes the thickening agent, or it may be*

Fruit soups offer such colour and variety – a rainbow of bright sunny hues or cooling pastels. They are refreshing, intriguing and a little unexpected. When you capture fruit at its peak of ripeness, the soup becomes the essence of melons, peaches or plums.

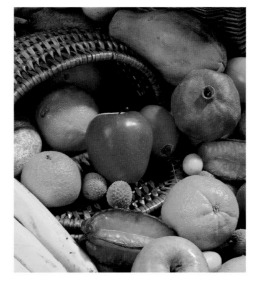

~.~.~.~.~.~.~.~.~.~

*"Ripe Apples drop about my head,*
*The Luscious Clusters of the Vine*
*Upon my mouth do crush their Wine;*
*The Nectaren, and curious Peach,*
*Into my hands themselves do reach;*
*Stumbling on Melons, as I pass."*

THE GARDEN
*Andrew Marvell, 1621–78*

~·~·~·~·~·~·~·~·~·~

Eternally popular citrus adds a refreshing tang to fruit soups, whether playing a major or minor role, while exotic fruits, such as papaya. Pomegranates and mango, or musky-scented melon, bring their tantalizing highly perfumed flavours.

combined with cream, yogurt or custard to achieve a smooth, luscious texture.

Many fruit soups have wine among the main ingredients. This can help to establish the balance of sweet and acidic flavours, particularly with ripe berries and other red fruits.

Fruit soups lend themselves to dramatic serving presentations. The colours themselves provide part of the dramatic element – most of these soups are jewel-like. But there is also the potential for originality in serving, such as decorating the side of the bowl – or the plate under it if using glass – with fresh flowers or serving from an ice bowl in which fruit and flowers are frozen.

# SUMMER BERRY SOUP

Croutons in a sweet soup? The combination of the fruit-soaked "croutons" atop luscious juicy berries rising from a pool of red berry purée provides a real dose of summer flavour.

**SERVES 4**

450g • 1lb ripe mixed berries
  (raspberries, blackberries,
  small strawberries,
  blueberries and
  blackcurrants), hulled
  or stemmed if necessary
4tbsp soft light brown sugar,
  or to taste

8 slices firm white bread
  or brioche
90ml • 3fl oz whipping cream
additional berries and mint
  leaves, to decorate
RASPBERRY PUREE
350g • 12oz ripe raspberries
40g • 1½oz icing sugar,
  or to taste

❶ Combine the mixed berries and brown sugar in a non-reactive saucepan and set over medium-low heat until the juices start to run, about 3–4 minutes. (The fruit should not be completely cooked.) Remove from the heat and leave to cool slightly. Strain the fruit, without pressing it down in the sieve, and reserve the juice in a large bowl.

❷ Line the bottom of four ramekins (about 175-ml/6-fl oz capacity) with rounds of greaseproof paper. Cut eight rounds from the bread the same diameter as the ramekins. Dip four of the bread rounds in the reserved juice and place in the bottom of the ramekins.

❸ Divide the fruit among the ramekins, pressing it down gently. Dip the remaining bread rounds in the reserved juice and place on top of the fruit. Cover the ramekins tightly and chill for at least 3 hours or overnight.

❹ For the raspberry purée, put the raspberries in a food processor fitted with a steel blade and process until smooth, then press through a sieve. Alternatively, work the berries through the fine blade of a food mill. Add the purée to the reserved juices from the fruit and add the icing sugar, plus more if you wish, and stir until it has dissolved. Cover and chill.

❺ To serve, unmould the ramekins into chilled shallow bowls and remove the greaseproof paper. Pour the raspberry purée around them and drizzle the cream into the purée. Place a few berries on the top of each serving with mint leaves to decorate.

# APRICOT SOUP

This bright, colourful dessert tastes of summer sunshine, even in winter. Using two kinds of apricots intensifies the flavour and you can make the purées up to one day ahead for easy assembly just before serving.

**SERVES 6**

115g • 4oz dried apricots
250ml • 8fl oz orange juice, plus more if needed
450g • 1lb fresh apricots, halved and stoned
4tbsp sweet white wine
1–2tbsp caster sugar
2tbsp apricot or peach liqueur
150ml • ¼pt crème fraîche, soured cream or fromage frais

❶ Combine the dried apricots and orange juice in a small non-reactive saucepan. Set over medium-low heat and simmer, covered, until the apricots are tender, about 35 minutes. Set aside to cool.
❷ Combine the fresh apricots, wine and sugar to taste in a medium-sized non-reactive saucepan and bring to the boil. Reduce the heat and simmer until the fruit is very tender, about 25 minutes. Transfer the fruit to a food processor fitted with a steel blade and process until smooth, then press through a sieve into a bowl. Stir in the liqueur and chill until cold.
❸ Scrape the dried apricot mixture into the food processor and process until smooth. Add the cream or fromage frais and pulse just until combined. The mixture should be about the same consistency as the cooked fresh apricots; add more orange juice if necessary. Transfer to a bowl and chill until cold.
❹ To serve, divide the fresh apricot mixture between chilled bowls and put a large spoonful of the dried apricot and cream mixture in the centre, dividing it evenly. Using the handle of a small spoon or a skewer, draw the dried apricot mixture out towards the edge of the bowl in five or six places to make a starburst pattern, curving at the outer edges, if you wish.

# CALIFORNIAN ICED FRUIT SOUP

This wine-based fruit soup is spectacular served in a fruit and flower ice bowl. You can make the decorative ice bowl several days in advance for convenience. Set it on a water-proof tray or a deep platter and surround with more flowers and leaves before filling with the fruit soup. The fresh fruit used in the soup can be varied according to seasonal availability.

**SERVES 6**

750ml • 1¼pt fruity white California wine
100g • 3½oz caster sugar, plus more if needed
2 unwaxed or scrubbed lemons
3 unwaxed or scrubbed oranges
2 ripe peaches, peeled and sliced, preferably
white-fleshed
225g • 8oz strawberries, halved if large
150g • 5oz blueberries or other small berries
decorative ice bowl, to serve (see page 121)

❶ Combine the wine and sugar in a glass or ceramic bowl. Stir to dissolve.
❷ Slice the lemons and one of the oranges thinly. Add them to the wine mixture and chill for several hours, stirring and pressing on the fruit occasionally.
❸ Peel and segment the remaining oranges over a bowl to catch the juice. Add the peaches, strawberries and blueberries, and stir to coat the fruit with orange juice. Taste and add sugar if needed. Cover and chill until serving.
❹ Strain the wine mixture into a serving bowl made of ice (or a glass serving bowl) and stir in the fruit and accumulated juices. Serve immediately.

# STRAWBERRY SOUP

At the height of the strawberry season, celebrate their perfection with this soup. If your berries are honey-sweet, you may not need any sugar!

**SERVES 6**

675g • 1½lb ripe strawberries, hulled
juice of 1 lemon
50g • 2oz caster sugar, or to taste
475ml • 16fl oz freshly squeezed, strained orange juice (about 4 oranges)
3 tbsp Cointreau or Kirsch
120ml • 4fl oz whipping cream
mint sprigs or strawberry leaves, to decorate

❶ Reserve 6 berries to decorate and put the remainder in a food processor fitted with a steel blade or in a blender. Add the lemon juice and sugar, depending on the sweetness of the berries and your taste, and purée until smooth.
❷ Sieve the purée into a large bowl and stir in the orange juice and Cointreau or Kirsch. Cover and chill until cold.
❸ Whip the cream until it forms soft peaks. Ladle the soup into chilled shallow bowls, preferably glass, and top each serving with a dollop of whipped cream. Decorate with the reserved berries and mint sprigs or strawberry leaves.

# SUNSET FRUIT SOUP

Intensely coloured exotic fruit purées arranged in adjoining bands make a dramatic presentation. Shallow glass soup plates or other very shallow plain dishes are most effective for serving this soup.

**SERVES 6–8**

50g • 2oz caster sugar
4tbsp water
1 small pineapple, peeled and cored, about 350g • 12oz
7 tbsp lime juice
1 large mango, about 450g • 1lb
1 large papaya, about 350g • 12oz

❶ Combine the sugar and water in a small saucepan and bring to the boil, stirring occasionally. Remove from the heat and let the syrup cool.
❷ Cut the pineapple into chunks and put in a food processor fitted with a steel blade with 1tbsp of the lime juice and 3tbsp of the sugar syrup. Purée until smooth. Scrape into a small bowl, cover and chill.
❸ Peel the mango. Cut down each side of the centre stone and put the flesh in the food processor (no need to wash it between puréeing each fruit), then cut off all the flesh adhering to the stone and add it to the workbowl. Add 3tbsp of the lime juice and 2tbsp of the sugar syrup and purée until smooth. Scrape into a small bowl, cover and chill.
❹ Halve the papaya and discard the seeds. Scoop the flesh into the food processor, leaving virtually none remaining on the skin. Add the remaining lime juice and sugar syrup and purée until smooth. Scrape into a small bowl, cover and chill.
❺ To serve, arrange the fruit purées in chilled shallow bowls or dishes in adjoining bands from lightest to darkest colours.

~.~.~.~.~.~.~.~.~

*VARIATION*
If any one of the fruits is unavailable, substitute yellow- or orange-fleshed melon.

~.~.~.~.~.~.~.~.~

# RUBY PLUM SOUP

This rich red soup is reminiscent of mulled wine, but with a pleasing fruity element. Using plums with red rather than yellow flesh will give the best colour. In frosty weather you could serve it hot, if you wish, in punch cups with a cinnamon stick in each.

**SERVES 8**

*1.25kg • 2½lb ripe red plums,
    halved and stoned*
*175ml • 6fl oz water*
*grated zest of 1 unwaxed or
    scrubbed lemon*
*3–4 allspice berries*
*5–6 cloves*

*5–6 peppercorns*
*600ml • 1pt ruby port*
*1–2tbsp runny honey*
*1 cinnamon stick*
*90–120ml • 3–4fl oz whipping
    cream, to decorate*

❶ Put the plums in a heavy saucepan with the water, lemon zest, allspice berries, cloves and peppercorns. Set over medium-low heat, cover and cook gently for about 20 minutes, or until the plums are very tender.

❷ Work the plums through the fine blade of a food mill set over a clean saucepan or press the mixture through a sieve; discard the spices.

❸ Stir in the port and honey to taste, add the cinnamon stick and bring to the boil. Reduce the heat to low and simmer for 15 minutes, stirring occasionally. Leave to cool, remove the cinnamon stick, cover and chill until cold.

❹ Ladle the soup into chilled bowls and drizzle two vertical lines of cream over the top of each serving. Using a cocktail stick or thin skewer, draw crosswise through the cream a little way into the soup, first in one direction, then in the other, wiping the stick between, to make a feather-like design. Alternatively, just drizzle the cream in random lines to decorate.

# MINTED MELON SOUP

There is nothing more refreshing than melon – it is light and cool, and prepared this way, it makes a pretty pastel picture. Only ripe melons will do for this cold soup, in fact the melon purée can be made from slightly overripe melons. Use whatever varieties of melons are available, as long as they are different colours. Serve this soup either as a starter or dessert.

**SERVES 4**

*1 large ripe green-fleshed*
  *melon, such as Honeydew,*
  *Galia or Ogen, about*
  *1kg • 2¼lb*
*5–6 mint leaves, plus more*
  *to decorate*
*150ml • ¼pt medium Muscat*
  *wine or white port*

*120ml • 4fl oz water*
*1–2tbsp lime juice (optional)*
*2–3tbsp caster sugar*
*½ large ripe orange-fleshed*
  *melon, such as Cantaloup,*
  *Charentais or Casaba,*
  *about 450g • 1lb*

❶ Discard the seeds from the green-fleshed melon and scoop the flesh into a blender or a food processor fitted with a steel blade. Add the mint, wine, water, lime juice, if using, and sugar. Purée until smooth and chill, covered.

❷ Discard the seeds of the orange-fleshed melon and, using a melon ball cutter, scoop out the flesh in small balls, or cut into cubes. Cover and chill.

❸ To serve, divide the melon purée among four chilled bowls. Arrange the melon balls on top, dividing them evenly, and decorate with mint.

*COOK'S TIP*

If you wish, use two smaller green-fleshed melons instead of 1 large one and serve the soup from the melon halves, cutting them in half, making a zig-zag edge for a more decorative effect. Try to find oval melons and cut them through the stem end instead of through the "equator", so the containers are as shallow as possible – otherwise the melon balls will be submerged.

# CITRUS SOUP

The richness of the smooth custard is a perfect background for the pleasantly sharp citrus fruit.

**SERVES 4**

*1 vanilla pod*
*300ml • ½pt full-fat milk*
*1 egg*
*2 egg yolks*
*65g • 2½oz caster sugar*

*1tbsp Cointreau, or other*
  *orange liqueur*
*2 large seedless oranges,*
  *unwaxed or scrubbed*
*1 ruby grapefruit*

❶ Put the vanilla pod and milk in a medium saucepan and bring just to the boil over medium-high heat, stirring frequently. Remove from the heat and cover. Leave to stand for 15–20 minutes and remove the vanilla pod.

❷ In a medium bowl, whisk the egg, egg yolks and 25g/1oz of the sugar for 2–3 minutes until thick and creamy. Whisk in the hot milk and return the mixture to the saucepan. With a wooden spoon, stir over medium-low heat until the custard begins to thicken and coat the back of the spoon (do not allow to boil or the custard may curdle). Immediately strain into a cold bowl set in a larger bowl of iced water and leave to cool, stirring occasionally. Stir in the Cointreau and chill, covered.

❸ With a vegetable peeler, remove the zest from one of the oranges in wide strips. Stack two or three strips at a time and slice into very thin matchstick slivers. Combine the remaining sugar and 5tbsp water in a small saucepan and bring to the boil, stirring occasionally. Add the orange zest, reduce the heat to low and simmer for 10 minutes. Remove from the heat and leave to cool.

❹ Peel the oranges and grapefruit, working over a bowl to catch the juices, and segment the fruit by cutting between the membranes. Add 3–4tbsp of the juice to the custard.

❺ Divide the custard among four chilled shallow bowls. Arrange the fruit in a starburst pattern on top and decorate with orange zest.

# CHOCOLATE-ORANGE SOUP

This luscious soup is a chocolate lover's dream come true. Use good quality Continental chocolate for the best flavour.

**SERVES 6**

300ml • 1pt milk
1 vanilla pod
200g • 7oz plain chocolate
3 egg yolks
25g • 1oz caster sugar
200ml • 7fl oz freshly squeezed,
strained orange juice
1tbsp Grand Marnier or other
    orange liqueur
120ml • 4fl oz whipping cream
shaved chocolate, to decorate

❶ Put the vanilla pod and milk in a medium saucepan and bring just to the boil over medium-high heat, stirring frequently. Remove from the heat and cover. Leave to stand for 15–20 minutes and remove the vanilla pod.

❷ Break the chocolate into small pieces and put in a food processor fitted with a steel blade. Process until finely ground.

❸ In a medium bowl, whisk the egg yolks and sugar for 2–3 minutes until thick and creamy. Whisk in the hot milk and return the mixture to the saucepan. With a wooden spoon, stir over medium-low heat until the custard begins to thicken and will coat the back of the spoon (do not allow it to boil or the custard may curdle).

❹ Immediately pour the custard over the chocolate in the food processor and process for 1 minute, or until the chocolate is melted and the mixture is homogenous. Strain into a cold bowl, stir in the orange juice and Grand Marnier and leave to cool, stirring occasionally. When cool, press cling film against the surface and chill until cold.

❺ Divide the chocolate soup between six chilled shallow bowls, swirl some cream in each and decorate with shaved chocolate.

~·~·~·~·~·~·~·~·~

*COOK'S TIP*
To make small shaved chocolate curls, hold a plain chocolate bar between your hands for a few seconds to soften it slightly. Using a vegetable peeler, scrape along the length of the edge. Chill the chocolate curls until needed for decorating.

~·~·~·~·~·~·~·~·~

# LEMON-WINE SOUP

This soup, based on a classic Italian dessert, *zabaglione*, features the fresh tangy flavour of lemon to balance the sweetness of the wine. The mixture triples in volume, so be sure to use a large bowl.

**SERVES 4**

*5 egg yolks*

*65g • 2½oz caster sugar, or more to taste*

*zest and juice of 1 medium unwaxed or scrubbed lemon*

*250ml • 8fl oz sweet white wine, such as Muscat or Sauternes*

*225g • 8oz fresh berries (raspberries, strawberries or blueberries), hulled or stemmed if necessary, or 2 ripe peaches, stoned, peeled and sliced*

❶ Half-fill a large saucepan with hot water and set over low heat (do not allow the water to boil). Put the egg yolks, sugar, lemon zest and juice in a large heatproof bowl which just fits into the pan without touching the water. Set the bowl over the water and, using an electric mixer at low speed or a balloon whisk, beat the mixture, gradually adding the wine. Continue cooking, beating constantly, until it is thick and fluffy, about 10 minutes.

❷ Remove from the heat and continue beating for about 4 minutes until the mixture is cooler.

❸ Chill, covered, until cold. To serve, stir the soup gently, divide among chilled glass bowls and arrange the fruit on top.

# CHAPTER SIX

# Cold Soups

COLD SOUPS ARE REFRESHING TO BOTH THE
COOK AND THE DINER ON SWELTERING
DAYS. THEY ARE PERFECT TO REVIVE FLAGGING
APPETITES WHEN TEMPERATURES SOAR AND MAKE
A COOLING START TO A LIGHT SUMMER MEAL – AS
SOOTHING AS SHADE IN THE SHIMMERING HEAT.
TO HELP YOU KEEP YOUR COOL IN THE KITCHEN
MANY OF THESE SOUPS FEATURE RAW INGRE-
DIENTS. THEY ALL OFFER VIBRANT FLAVOURS AND
CREATIVE COMBINATIONS TO RENEW THE JADED
PALATE AND WILTING SPIRIT.

# COLD SOUPS

*T*he following sampler of cold soups is drawn from diverse origins, but many are from countries with hot climates. This seems logical, notwithstanding a tradition of steaming hot, spicy soups in these countries, as well.

Cold soups are satisfying in so many ways. The tangy union of tomato and citrus, the icy crunch of cucumber – what could be more refreshing? These soups are designed to cool you down without filling you up.

Flavours tend to fade when chilled, so season more liberally than when preparing hot soups. More forthright flavours are appropriate in soups where garlic or spices predominate, but you

~.~.~.~.~.~.~.~.~

*"I live on good soup, not
on fine words."*

LES FEMMES SAVANTES
*Moliére, 1622–73*

~.~.~.~.~.~.~.~.~

Cold soups are most often served in warm weather when vegetables are at their peak. Garden fresh vegetables with their full ripe flavour are the best choice for these soups because they won't fade too much when chilled, but generous seasoning is also called for.

*will probably also need to use basic seasonings like salt and herbs more generously than usual.*

*Many soups traditionally served hot are equally delicious cold. Puréed vegetable soups, in particular, offer this versatility – in fact, the selection in this chapter is entirely vegetable-based with meat or seafood for embellishment. Try a spoonful before reheating a soup destined for serving hot to see if you like it cold. Use your imagination and experiment.*

*Serving cold soups really cold is worth the small effort required. Chill them well. If time is short or the weather is hot, set the container in a bowl of cracked ice prior to ladling the soup out. You can even use this system for individual servings, setting a small bowl inside a larger bowl of finely crushed ice, but at least serve the soup in ice-cold bowls or glasses. Put them in the freezer briefly if there is room. Some of these soups are customarily served with ice cubes floating in them.*

# RED PEPPER SOUP *with* PRAWNS

The sunny Mediterranean flavours of this cold, refreshing soup will make you think you are sipping it on the Riviera.

**SERVES 6**

| | |
|---|---|
| *6 large red peppers* | *350ml • 12fl oz garlic* |
| *1tbsp vegetable oil* | *vegetable stock (see page 17),* |
| *450g • 1lb leeks, thinly sliced* | *or more water* |
| *1 large onion, halved and* | *fresh lemon juice, to taste* |
| *thinly sliced* | *6tbsp soured cream or crème* |
| *½ fennel bulb, thinly sliced* | *fraîche, for serving* |
| *¼tsp dried chilli flakes* | *180g • 6oz small peeled* |
| *250ml • 8fl oz water* | *prawns, to garnish* |
| *salt and freshly ground pepper* | |

❶ Preheat the oven to 200°C/400°F/Gas 6. Put the peppers in a baking dish and roast for about 55 minutes, turning a quarter-turn every 15 minutes, until the peppers are wrinkly and the skin has begun to darken. Put them in a plastic storage box or bag, close tightly and leave to steam for 30 minutes. Halve the peppers and remove the core, seeds and skin. Roughly chop the pepper flesh.

❷ Heat the oil in a large saucepan over medium heat. Add the leeks and onion, and cook, covered, until just softened, about 5 minutes. Stir in the fennel, chilli flakes and roasted peppers. Add the water and a little salt and pepper, and simmer over medium-low heat for about 30 minutes, until all the vegetables are tender.

❸ Transfer the vegetables and cooking liquid to a blender or a food processor fitted with a steel blade and purée until smooth.

❹ In a bowl, combine the purée and stock or additional water, leave to cool, then cover and refrigerate until cold. When ready to serve, taste and adjust the seasoning and add a few drops of lemon juice. Ladle the soup into cold bowls or soup plates, put a dollop of soured cream or *crème fraîche* on each and arrange the prawns on the cream, dividing them evenly.

~.~.~.~.~.~.~.~.~.~

*TO DRINK*
A rosé from
Provence or well-
chilled Pineau des
Charentes.

~.~.~.~.~.~.~.~.~.~

# CORDOBAN GAZPACHO

*(Salmorejo)*

This cold soup from Cordoba, *Salmorejo*, is refreshing on a hot day. The recipe is adapted from the soup served at El Caballo Rojo, a fine restaurant in the old section of the city, and is one of many versions of gazpacho found in Andalucía. A blender gives a smooth, creamy texture and saves time on preparation. If it is necessary to use a food processor, it is best to peel and deseed the tomatoes first and sieve the soup after puréeing.

**SERVES 6–8**

| | |
|---|---|
| *275g • 10oz stale French bread* | *6tbsp extra-virgin olive oil* |
| *1kg • 2¼lb ripe tomatoes,* | *salt* |
| *washed and cored* | TO GARNISH |
| *1 small onion, quartered* | *2 hard-boiled eggs, sliced* |
| *2 garlic cloves, crushed* | *75g • 3oz sliced Spanish ham,* |
| *10ml • 2tsp sherry vinegar* | *cut in slivers* |

❶ Trim the crusts from the bread, cut into thick slices and cover with cold water. Remove the bread, squeeze out the water and put the bread in a blender.

❷ Cut the tomatoes into quarters and add them to the soaked bread with the onion, garlic and vinegar.

❸ Blend the ingredients for several minutes until completely puréed, scraping the sides of the blender as necessary.

❹ Slowly add the olive oil through the hole in the top. If you wish, thin the soup with a little iced water (the soup should be thick). Season to taste with salt.

❺ Chill the soup thoroughly. Ladle into chilled bowls and garnish with slices of egg and slivers of ham.

~.~.~.~.~.~.~.~.~.~

*COOK'S TIP*
To peel tomatoes, remove the
core and cut a shallow cross in the
base, cover with boiling water for
10 seconds, drain, then immerse in cold
water and drain again. Cut in half
and scrape out the seeds into a sieve
to extract the juice. Add the
juice to the soup.

~.~.~.~.~.~.~.~.~.~

# CHILLED GREEN PEA SOUP

This soup is a stunning bright green colour. It is simple to make and quite tasty using frozen peas, but if you are able to find fresh-picked young garden peas, you are in for a real gourmet treat.

**SERVES 6**

| | |
|---|---|
| *15g • ½oz butter* | *150ml • ¼pt whipping cream* |
| *4 shallots, finely chopped* | *2tbsp chopped fresh mint* |
| *800g • 1¾lb shelled fresh peas* | *12–18 small mangetout,* |
| *or thawed frozen peas* | *blanched and chilled, to* |
| *1l • 1¾pt water* | *garnish* |
| *salt and freshly ground pepper* | |

❶ Melt the butter in a large saucepan over medium-low heat. Add the shallots and cook, stirring occasionally, until they begin to soften, about 5 minutes.

❷ Add the peas and water. Season with salt and a little pepper. Simmer covered, stirring occasionally, until the vegetables are tender, about 12 minutes for frozen or young fresh peas, or up to 18 minutes for large or older peas.

❸ Transfer the solids to a blender or a food processor fitted with a steel blade. Add some of the cooking liquid and purée until smooth, working in batches if necessary. Sieve into a bowl with the remaining cooking liquid, leave to stand until cool, cover and refrigerate until cold.

❹ Using an electric mixer or whisk, whip the cream in a chilled bowl until soft peaks form. Stir in the mint.

❺ Thin the soup with a little cold water, if needed, and adjust the seasoning. Ladle into cold soup plates and garnish each with a dollop of cream and 2–3 mangetout.

~.~.~.~.~.~.~.~.~.~

*COOK'S TIP*
You will need
2.25–2.5kg/5–6lb
fresh peas in the pod
to obtain 800g/1¾lb
shelled peas.

~.~.~.~.~.~.~.~.~.~

# CUCUMBER COOLER

This soup is so refreshing – cool as the proverbial cucumber with a subtle hint of mint.

**SERVES 6**

| | |
|---|---|
| *2 large cucumbers* | *30ml • 2tbsp finely chopped* |
| *275g • 10oz plain yogurt* | *fresh mint* |
| *(preferably Greek-style)* | *salt and freshly ground pepper* |
| *175ml • 6fl oz buttermilk* | *fresh lemon juice, to taste* |
| *1–2 garlic cloves, very finely* | *mint leaves, to garnish* |
| *minced* | |

❶ Cut 12 thin slices from one of the cucumbers and reserve, covered, for garnishing. Peel the cucumbers, slice lengthwise and scoop out the seeds with a small sharp spoon.

❷ Grate the cucumbers and transfer to a large bowl. Stir in the yogurt, buttermilk, garlic and mint. Season to taste with salt and pepper and a few drops of lemon juice.

❸ Refrigerate until thoroughly chilled, about 1 hour. Ladle into chilled soup plates and garnish with the reserved cucumber slices and mint leaves.

# COLD BORSCHT

There is no single definite recipe for Borscht, the popular Eastern European peasant soup. In fact, there seem to be to almost limitless variations – some with meat, some with beans, some mainly cabbage, others mainly beetroots. This meatless version offers a balanced combination of vegetable flavours that meld when chilled.

**SERVES 6**

*½ medium red cabbage, cored*
*and coarsely chopped*
*1tbsp vegetable oil*
*1 large onion, chopped*
*1 large leek, split and sliced*
*1 large carrot, thinly sliced*
*1 medium parsnip, thinly sliced*
*150ml • ¼pt red wine*
*1.2l • 2pt chicken stock or*
*water, plus more if needed*

*6 medium beetroot, peeled*
*and cubed*
*4 tomatoes, peeled, deseeded*
*and coarsely chopped*
*bay leaf*
*1tsp sherry vinegar or red*
*wine vinegar*
*soured cream or yogurt,*
*to serve*
*chopped fresh dill, to garnish*

❶ Cover the cabbage with cold water. Set over high heat, bring to the boil and boil for 3 minutes. Drain.

❷ Heat the oil in a large saucepan over medium-low heat and add the onion and leek. Cover and sweat the vegetables until soft, about 5 minutes, stirring occasionally. Add the carrot, parsnip, blanched cabbage and wine. Bring to the boil and add the stock or water, beetroots, tomatoes and bay leaf. Bring back to the boil, reduce the heat and simmer until all the vegetables are tender, about 1¼ hours.

❸ Remove the bay leaf and, using a slotted spoon, transfer the solids to a blender or a food processor fitted with a steel blade, working in batches if necessary. Add some of the cooking liquid and purée until smooth. Sieve the solids and any remaining cooking liquid into a large bowl. Stir in the vinegar, leave to cool and refrigerate until cold.

❹ If you wish, thin the soup with water or more stock. Season to taste with salt and pepper, and add a little more vinegar, if liked. Ladle into chilled soup bowls or plates, top each with a dollop of soured cream or yogurt and sprinkle lightly with dill.

~.~.~.~.~.~.~.~.~.~

*TO DRINK*
Sparkling
red wine.

~·~·~·~·~·~·~·~·~·~

# LAVENDER VICHYSSOISE

Use blue potatoes with deeply coloured flesh for this soup. If made from pale blue potatoes it will be grey, not pale purple. The flavour of lavender is pervasive, so a tiny amount is sufficient.

**SERVES 6–8**

| | |
|---|---|
| *15g • ½oz butter* | *pinch of lavender flowers* |
| *1 large shallot (mauve if possible), finely chopped* | *salt and white pepper* |
| *450g • 1lb blue potatoes, cubed* | *150ml • ¼pt whipping cream* |
| *1.2l • 2pt chicken stock* | *3tbsp chopped fresh chives, to garnish* |
| *3 large leeks, white part only, split and thinly sliced* | *chive flowers, to garnish* |

❶ Melt the butter in a large saucepan over medium heat. Add the shallot and cook until just softened, about 5 minutes. Add the potatoes and stock, and bring to the boil over high heat. Reduce the heat to medium-low and simmer for about 25 minutes, stirring occasionally.

❷ When the potatoes are just tender when pierced, stir in the leeks. Add the lavender and a little salt and pepper. Simmer for 10–15 minutes longer until the vegetables are soft and tender, stirring occasionally.

❸ Transfer the solids to a blender or a food processor fitted with a steel blade. Add some of the cooking liquid and purée until smooth, working in batches if necessary.

❹ Strain the mixture into a bowl, pressing firmly with the back of a spoon to extract as much liquid as possible. Stir in the cream and, if the soup seems too thick, thin it with a little more stock or water. Leave to cool and refrigerate until cold. Ladle into chilled bowls or cups and garnish with chives and chive flowers.

~·~·~·~·~·~·~·~·~·~

*COOK'S TIP*
If blue (purple-fleshed) potatoes are difficult to find, use white potatoes and peel them before cooking.

~·~·~·~·~·~·~·~·~·~

# ICED ALMOND *and* GARLIC SOUP

This recipe, *Ajo Blanco de Málaga*, dates from the tenth century when the Moors inhabited Andalucía. It is one of numerous versions of gazpacho popular all over Spain. This version is typical of Málaga.

**SERVES 4**

| | |
|---|---|
| *150g • 5oz soft white breadcrumbs, made from flavourful homemade-style bread* | *pinch of salt* |
| | *2tsp sherry vinegar* |
| | *6tbsp extra-virgin olive oil* |
| *200g • 7oz blanched almonds, lightly toasted* | *750ml • 1¼pt water* |
| | *115g • 4oz seedless white grapes, to garnish* |
| *2 garlic cloves, minced* | |

❶ Soak the breadcrumbs in cold water to cover for 5 minutes.

❷ Put the almonds, garlic and salt in a food processor fitted with a steel blade and process until the nuts are finely ground. Strain the breadcrumbs, pressing with the back of a spoon to extract more water, and add to the almond mixture and process until pasty.

❸ Add the vinegar and, with the machine running, pour the oil through the feed tube, then slowly pour in the water, stopping to scrape down the sides several times. Sieve into a bowl and refrigerate until very cold.

❹ Ladle over ice cubes into a chilled tureen or soup plates and garnish with the grapes.

*Lilian's Soup*

# ICED TOMATO *and* ORANGE SOUP

This lean, flavourful soup depends on ripe tomatoes. Use seasonal sun-ripened tomatoes at their peak – plum tomatoes are best.

**SERVES 4**

*2tsp olive oil*
*1 large sweet onion, chopped*
*1 medium carrot, chopped*
*1.25kg · 2½lb ripe tomatoes, cored and quartered*
*1 orange, thinly sliced (unwaxed or scrubbed)*
*bouquet garni (thyme and*
*marjoram sprigs and bay leaf)*
*250ml · 8fl oz water*
*salt and freshly ground pepper*
*120ml · 4fl oz fresh orange juice*
*mint sprigs, to garnish*

❶ Heat the olive oil in a large non-reactive saucepan or flameproof casserole over medium heat. Add the onion and carrot, and cook for 4–5 minutes, stirring occasionally, until the onion is just softened.

❷ Add the tomatoes, orange and bouquet garni. Reduce the heat to medium-low, cover and simmer for about 40 minutes, stirring once or twice, until the vegetables are very soft.

❸ Work the tomato mixture through a food mill fitted with a fine blade set over a bowl. Add the orange juice and season to taste with salt and pepper. Sieve the soup, leave to cool, cover and refrigerate until cold. Serve in tumblers, with ice cubes if you like, and garnish with mint sprigs.

*Sieve through clean cloth. (muslin)*

*In bowl: Finely chopped cucumber, beetroot sprouts, iced basil cubes, olive oil caviar. Put in iced bowls, pour soup at table.*

# COLD AVOCADO SOUP

This spicy soup is like a guacamole that you can drink. The best avocados to use are the very large ones with bright green skin, such as Lula or Ettinger varieties. Haas avocados, smaller with dark pebbly skin, will do but they discolour quickly and can darken the soup.

**SERVES 4–6**

*1l · 1¾pt chicken stock*
*6 garlic cloves, chopped*
*bouquet garni (parsley stems, coriander stems, thyme and marjoram sprigs)*
*2 large avocados, about 450g · 1lb each, ripe but not soft*
*3–4tbsp fresh lime juice*
*2–3tsp chopped jalapeño*
*chillies*
*250ml · 8fl oz soured cream*
*salt*
*Tabasco sauce*
*2 plum tomatoes, peeled, deseeded, finely chopped and drained*
*3 spring onions, finely chopped*
*2–3tbsp chopped fresh coriander leaves*

❶ Combine the stock and garlic in a saucepan and bring to the boil over high heat, skimming off any foam that rises to the surface. Add the bouquet garni, reduce the heat to low and simmer for 30 minutes, or until the stock tastes of garlic. Strain into a bowl, leave to cool and then refrigerate until cold. Remove any congealed fat.

❷ Shortly before serving, cut the avocados in half, discard the stones and scoop the flesh into a blender or a food processor fitted with a steel blade. Add the lime juice and jalapeños. Remove any congealed fat from the stock, add half of it and purée until smooth, scraping down the sides as necessary. Add as much of the remaining stock as the capacity of the blender or processor permits and process to combine.

❸ Transfer the mixture to a large bowl. Stir in any remaining stock and a third of the soured cream. Season with salt and Tabasco to taste, adding more lime juice if you like. Ladle into chilled small bowls or glass punch cups. Dollop on the remaining soured cream and sprinkle each serving with chopped tomatoes, spring onions and coriander, dividing them evenly.

~·~·~·~·~·~·~·~·~·~

*TO DRINK*
Margaritas or ice-cold
Aquavit.

~·~·~·~·~·~·~·~·~·~

CHAPTER SEVEN

# Clear Soups

SHIMMERING LUCID LIQUID, LIGHT AND
BRIMMING WITH FLAVOUR, LIFTS THE
SPIRIT AND TEASES THE APPETITE. PERFECT CON-
SOMMÉS HAVE LONG BEEN CONSIDERED THE TRUE
TEST OF A CHEF'S SKILL AND, MADE IN THE
TRADITIONAL WAY, THEY REQUIRE A CERTAIN
AMOUNT OF DEDICATION. BUT MANY OF THE
CLEAR SOUPS WHICH FOLLOW ARE SIMPLER
CREATIONS, UNITING THE BEST QUALITIES OF
CLASSIC CUISINE AND THE REQUIREMENTS OF
MODERN LIVING.

# CLEAR SOUPS

P urists would argue that only consommés can be classed as
clear soups. Those are here, and they are worth making.
But I take a broader view and so here, too, are soups which are
essentially light broths, enveloping and providing the backdrop for
other ingredients in them.

The liquid element is the most important, and all these soups
must be made with flavourful homemade stock. Seize the moment
when you have good rich stock available.

The additional ingredients are really embellishments for the
stock. In classic French cuisine, these are called garnishes, and they
offer the opportunity for endless variety. Consommés, in particular,
have a traditional repertoire of embellishments, such as a
sprinkling of herbs, finely diced or slivered vegetables or pieces of

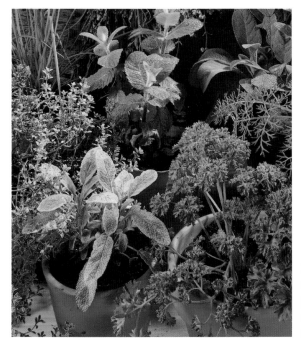

~.~.~.~.~.~.~.~.~

*"I believe I was once
considerably scandalized
by her declaring that clear
soup was a more
important factor in life
than a clear conscience."*

Saki (H. H. Munro)
*1870–1916*

~.~.~.~.~.~.~.~.~

Light and limpid clear soups need simple, colourful garnishes such as fresh herbs or bright slivers of vegetables to bring an added dimension of flavour and highlight their clarity.

*egg custard cut into pretty shapes, each giving the soup a different name. A clear, shimmering, flavourful consommé is considered a test of culinary skill and a worthy accomplishment.*

*In principle, all of these soups could utilize clarified stock, but if the stock is relatively limpid – clear enough to see what is in the soup – clarification is only necessary for consommés. Even then, if you "brew" the stock slowly, it may be acceptably clear.*

*Serve these soups in a way that accentuates their clarity and allows any ingredients in them to be seen. Glass bowls or white porcelain are ideal.*

*A clear soup makes a perfect starter – light and not too filling to prevent the enjoyment of what is to follow. Servings are generally small and the yield calculated in the recipes reflects this. Naturally these soups can be made more substantial by adding more embellishments and serving in larger portions, if you wish.*

# BEEF CONSOMME *with* PARMESAN PROFITEROLES

Consommé is a classic starter before a rich, elaborate meal, as it stimulates the palate and whets the appetite without filling. The method for clarifying stock is the same for any kind, but the ingredients to flavour the consommé are chosen to suit each one. Garnishes also vary; they should be a light adjunct offering a bit of contrast and novelty.

### SERVES 6

*2l • 3½pt strong fat-free beef stock*
*350–450g • 12–16oz very lean minced beef*
*2 leeks, finely chopped*
*1 onion, finely chopped*
*1 carrot, finely chopped*
*1 tomato, finely chopped*
*1 small bunch fresh parsley, finely chopped*
*10ml • 2tsp dried tarragon*
*2 egg whites*
*Parmesan profiteroles (see page 123), to garnish*

❶ Put the minced beef in a large saucepan with the leeks, onion, carrot, tomato, parsley and dried tarragon. Add the egg whites, mix to combine and stir in the stock. Set over high heat and stir almost continuously as the mixture comes to the boil. When it begins to tremble, reduce the heat to low and simmer very gently, without stirring or disturbing it, for 30 minutes. Carefully lift off about half of the solid covering, using a slotted spoon, and ladle the clarified stock through a sieve lined with damp muslin into a saucepan. (Discard the solid matter.) Blot any grease from the surface with paper towels.
❷ Bring the consommé just to simmering, ladle into warmed soup plates or bowls and garnish with Parmesan profiteroles, or use other garnishes if you prefer (see box, below).

#### GARNISHES FOR CONSOMMES
*chopped herbs*
*finely diced root vegetables, parboiled and drained*
*julienne strips of carrot, celery, leeks or spring onions, parboiled and drained*
*finely diced, peeled and deseeded tomato*
*thinly sliced or diced peppers (roasted, peeled and deseeded)*
*thinly sliced mushrooms*
*diced or sliced truffle*
*thin eggy crêpes made with chopped herbs, sliced into strips*
*thin ribbons of spinach or leaf lettuce*
*strips of cooked beef, chicken, ham or other meat*
*cooked rice, barley or noodles*
*cooked filled pasta*

# GAME BIRD CONSOMME *with* POACHED QUAIL EGGS

This is not a classic consommé, as it is not clarified. Cooking it slowly is an easy and effective method to achieve a relatively clear stock and retain the delicate flavour that would be lost in the clarification process.

### SERVES 4

*1 large game bird carcass, such as pheasant or duck, or 3–4 small ones, such as pigeon or quail, raw or cooked and trimmed of excess fat*
*1 large onion, quartered*
*2 carrots, coarsely chopped*
*1 parsnip, coarsely chopped*
*1 leek, sliced*
*2–4 garlic cloves, crushed*
*1tbsp black peppercorns*
*bouquet garni (thyme sprigs, parsley stems, tarragon or sage leaves and bay leaf)*
*750ml • 1¼pt cold chicken stock*
*8 quail eggs*
*salt (optional)*
*2–3tbsp dry sherry*
*fresh chervil or flat-leafed parsley, to garnish*

❶ Put the carcass(es), onion, carrots, parsnip, leek, garlic, peppercorns and bouquet garni in a Dutch oven or large heavy saucepan. Add the stock and enough cold water to cover the ingredients by 2.5cm/1in. Bring slowly to the boil over medium heat, skimming the foam that rises to the surface often. Reduce the heat to low and simmer for 1½–2 hours. Strain the stock through a sieve lined with damp muslin into a bowl and if any meat can be picked off the carcass, reserve it. Cool the stock and chill for several hours or overnight. Skim off any congealed fat and blot the surface with a paper towel to remove any remaining fat.
❷ Bring a small pan of salted water to the boil and poach the quail eggs, a few at a time, for 2–3 minutes, or until done as you like them. Remove with a slotted spoon to a bowl of tepid water to stop further cooking. Trim off any untidy bits of white.
❸ Bring the stock just to the boil and reduce the heat to medium-low. Taste and season with a little salt, if needed, and stir in the sherry. If the stock is bland, reduce it slightly with a fresh bouquet garni.
❹ Place the eggs in warmed shallow soup plates, ladle over the consommé and garnish with chervil or parsley leaves.

# WONTON SOUP

This light and delicious soup has universal appeal. The small dumplings are a popular snack in China and are sometimes served crisply fried.

**SERVES 6**

| | |
|---|---|
| *15g • ½oz dried Oriental mushrooms* | *pinch of Oriental 5-spice powder (optional)* |
| *225g • 8oz lean boneless pork, cubed* | *1tsp soy sauce* |
| *25g • 1oz fresh spinach leaves* | *1 egg, separated* |
| *2–3 spring onions, coarsely chopped* | *24 wonton wrappers* |
| *1 garlic clove, minced* | *2l • 3½pt chicken stock* |
| | *finely slivered spring onions, to garnish* |

❶ Put the dried mushrooms in a small bowl and cover with boiling water. Leave to soak for about 20 minutes. Drain and blot dry. Chop finely.

❷ Combine the pork, spinach leaves, spring onions and garlic in a food processor fitted with a steel blade and pulse until finely chopped, or finely chop with a large knife. Add the 5-spice powder, if using, the soy sauce and egg yolk, and pulse, or stir, until mixed. Beat the egg white with 1tsp water in a small bowl.

❸ Place 6 wonton wrappers on a work surface. Put a rounded teaspoonful of filling in the centre of each wrapper. Brush egg white around the filling. Bring the edges together to enclose the filling and twist, pressing together to secure. Continue filling the remaining wonton wrappers.

❹ Bring a large quantity of salted water to the boil. Drop in half the wontons, bring back to the boil and cook for 3–4 minutes until they have come to the surface and the wonton dough is tender. Drain on a clean tea towel and cook the remainder.

❺ Meanwhile, bring the stock to the boil in a large saucepan. Divide the wontons between 6 warmed bowls, sprinkle with spring onions and ladle the hot stock over them.

# ROASTED GARLIC SOUP

This soup has a mellow, almost smoky, garlic flavour that makes it immensely satisfying yet very light. A strong well-flavoured stock is essential and it should be relatively clear, to see the croutons. It is inspired by the Mediterranean peasant soups found in France, Italy, Spain and Portugal.

**SERVES 4**

*1 large head large-clove garlic, about 100g • 3½oz*
*1l • 1¾pt chicken or beef stock*

*2–3 slices white bread, crusts trimmed*
*finely chopped fresh parsley, to garnish*

❶ Preheat the oven to 200°C/400°F/Gas 6. Wrap the garlic, whole, in foil and bake for about 40 minutes until very soft.
❷ Bring the stock just to the boil over medium heat. Remove and set aside 3 cloves of the garlic, put the rest of the head into the stock and press with a wooden spoon to crush it lightly. Reduce the heat to low and simmer gently, partially covered, for 30 minutes, or until the stock has taken on the flavour of the garlic.
❸ Cut the bread into 12 squares or diamond shapes about 3cm/1¼in on each side. Place on a baking sheet and toast the bread lightly. Squeeze out the garlic from the reserved garlic cloves and spread on the croutons.
❹ Place the croutons in the bottom of warmed soup plates. Strain the soup to remove the garlic and ladle it over the croutons, dividing evenly between the soup plates. Sprinkle with parsley and serve.

# TORTILLA SOUP

The crunchy tortilla strips bring a satisfying element of contrast to this light soup. If you prefer, pass them separately, along with chopped spring onions and coriander leaves. In Mexico, small cubes of cheese are sometimes added.

**SERVES 6**

*2tsp vegetable oil, plus more for frying*
*1 small onion, finely chopped*
*3 garlic cloves, minced*
*2l • 3½pt chicken stock*
*¼tsp dried chilli flakes*
*¼tsp each dried thyme and oregano*
*fresh parsley and coriander stems*
*bay leaf*

*salt*
*6–8 corn tortillas*
*5 tomatoes (preferably plum), peeled, deseeded and diced*
*1 avocado, stoned, peeled and diced*
To Garnish
*3–4 spring onions, finely chopped*
*2–3tbsp chopped fresh coriander leaves*

❶ Heat the oil in a large saucepan over medium heat. Add the onion and garlic, and cook until softened, 3–4 minutes. Stir in the stock and add the chilli flakes, herbs and a little salt. Simmer, partially covered, for about 30 minutes, stirring occasionally.
❷ Stack the tortillas and cut into strips 1.25cm/½in wide and 5cm/2in long. In a medium-sized frying pan, add oil to a depth of about 1.25cm/½in. Set over medium-high heat and when the oil begins to smoke, fry the tortilla strips in batches until crisp and lightly browned, about 1 minute. Remove with a slotted spoon and drain on paper towels. Keep warm in a slow oven.
❸ Strain the soup into a clean saucepan, stir in the tomatoes and simmer gently over low heat for 5 minutes, or until heated through. Add the avocado, cook for 1–2 minutes longer and ladle the soup into warmed bowls. Garnish with tortilla strips, spring onions and coriander leaves.

# SEAFOOD RAVIOLI *in* BOUILLON

These filled pasta pillows are easy to make and lend themselves to all sorts of fillings. Vary the seafood in the filling according to what is available, using cooked fish, clams or scallops, chopped, to make about 200–225g/7–8oz seafood.

**SERVES 8**

*1.5l • 2¾pt seafood stock*
*fresh coriander leaves, to*
*    garnish*
PASTA
*150g • 5oz strong plain flour,*
*    plus more for dusting*
*¼tsp salt*
*1 whole egg*
*1 egg, separated*
*1tsp olive oil*
*30–45ml • 2–3tbsp cold water*

FILLING
*75g • 3oz crab meat*
*115g • 4oz small peeled cooked*
*    prawns, chopped and well*
*    drained*
*2tsp finely chopped parsley*
*2tsp finely chopped fresh*
*    coriander leaves*
*1tsp finely chopped chives*
*freshly ground black pepper*
*lemon juice*
*4tsp whipping cream*

❶ For the pasta, put the flour and salt into a food processor fitted with a steel blade and pulse to combine. In a small bowl, beat together the egg, egg yolk, oil and 2tbsp of the water. With the machine running, pour in the mixture and process until it forms a ball which leaves the bowl virtually clean. If the dough seems crumbly, add the remaining water; if it seems sticky, add 1–2tbsp flour and continue kneading until it forms a ball. Wrap and chill for at least 30 minutes. Set aside the egg white in a small dish.

❷ For the filling, combine the crab meat, prawns and herbs in a bowl. Season with pepper and a few drops of lemon juice, and stir in the cream until well mixed.

❸ Divide the pasta dough into quarters and keep the remaining dough wrapped while you roll out one quarter. Using a pasta machine and starting on the thickest setting, roll through the dough, each time on successively thinner settings. (The dough should be thin enough to begin to see through but not tear easily.) Lay the strip of dough on a lightly floured work surface and cut in half. Place 4 rounded teaspoonfuls of filling at even intervals along one half. Brush around the filling with egg white and lay the remaining half strip over the top. Press gently but firmly to seal. Cut out with a 7.5-cm/3-in round cutter or cut into squares. Arrange the ravioli in one layer on a baking sheet dusted generously with flour and repeat with the remaining dough. Leave the

ravioli to dry in a cool place for about 15 minutes or chill for 1–2 hours.

❹ Bring a large quantity of salted water to the boil and cook the ravioli, a few at a time, until the pasta is just tender, about 3 minutes. Drain on a clean tea towel while cooking the remainder.

❺ Meanwhile, bring the stock to the boil in a large saucepan. Divide the ravioli between warmed shallow soup plates, ladle over the stock and garnish with fresh coriander leaves.

# LEMON EGG DROP SOUP

*(Avegolemono)*

This traditional Greek soup has its counterparts in Italy and China. It is essentially simple, but depends on a rich flavourful stock. Fish stock may be used instead of chicken, and rice is often added.

**SERVES 4**

*1l • 1¾pt chicken stock*
*2 eggs*
*3tbsp fresh lemon juice,*
*    or to taste*

*salt and freshly ground pepper*
*2tbsp chopped fresh parsley*

❶ Bring the stock to the boil in a large saucepan over medium-high heat. Reduce the heat to medium-low so it just simmers.

❷ In a small bowl or measuring jug, beat the eggs and lemon juice with a fork until combined. Season with salt and pepper.

❸ Beat a few tablespoons of the stock into the egg mixture, then very slowly pour the mixture into the soup, whisking slowly and constantly with the fork until the egg is set.

❹ Taste and adjust the seasoning, adding more lemon juice if you wish. Ladle the soup into warm bowls and sprinkle with parsley.

# Tarragon Chicken Consomme
## *with* Chicken Quenelles

A richly flavoured, sparkling clear consommé is considered a true indicator of culinary skill. Although it is relatively expensive and time-consuming, it is worth making the effort at least once. Start with strong homemade stock, as the clarification process steals some of the flavour, in spite of the additional flavouring ingredients. Reduce your stock, if necessary, to concentrate the flavour before beginning.

**SERVES 6**

*1 skinless boneless chicken
    breast, about 200g • 7oz*
*2 small leeks, finely chopped*
*1 onion, finely chopped*
*1 celery stick, finely chopped*
*3–4 sprigs fresh parsley, finely
    chopped*
*2tsp dried tarragon*
*2 egg whites*
*2l • 3½pt strong fat-free
    chicken stock*
*chopped fresh tarragon leaves,
    to garnish*

CHICKEN QUENELLES
*1 skinless boneless chicken
    breast, well chilled, about
    200g • 7oz*
*1 egg white*
*1tbsp chopped fresh tarragon*
*4tbsp whipping cream, well
    chilled*
*salt and freshly ground pepper*
*freshly grated nutmeg*

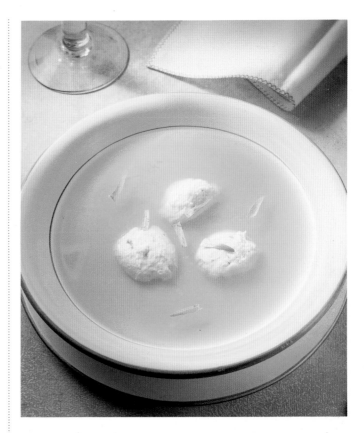

❶ Finely chop the chicken breast in a food processor or by hand. Put in a large saucepan with the leeks, onion, celery, parsley and dried tarragon. Add the egg whites, mix to combine and stir in the stock. Set over high heat and stir almost continuously as the mixture comes to the boil. When it begins to tremble, reduce the heat to low and simmer very gently, without stirring or disturbing it, for 30 minutes. Carefully lift off about a third of the solid covering, using a slotted spoon, and ladle the clarified stock through a sieve lined with damp muslin. (Discard the solid matter.)

❷ For the chicken quenelles, cut the chicken breast into large pieces, put in a food processor fitted with a steel blade and process until smooth. Add the egg white and tarragon, and mix until combined. Add the cream by spoonfuls. Do not overprocess or the mixture will become warm and the cream will not be readily absorbed. Season generously, add a pinch of nutmeg and chill.

❸ Bring a pan of salted water to the simmer. Using two teaspoons, shape the chicken mixture into small ovals and drop into the water a few at a time. Poach for about 2 minutes until they float and feel firm to the touch. Drain on clean tea towels.

❹ Bring the consommé just to the boil over medium-high heat. Divide the quenelles between warmed shallow soup plates, ladle over the consommé and sprinkle with a little chopped tarragon.

CHAPTER EIGHT

# *Garnishes and Accompaniments*

MOST SOUPS BENEFIT FROM EMBELLISH-
MENT AND IT IS THE PERFECT ARENA
TO GIVE YOUR IMAGINATION FREE REIN. THE
OPTIONS FOR GARNISHES AND ACCOMPANIMENTS
ARE SO BROAD AND FLEXIBLE THAT ALMOST ANY-
THING GOES. THEY CAN BE AS SIMPLE AS A FEW
FRESH HERBS, AS ARTISTIC AS A FEATHERY DESIGN
IN CREAM, AS SATISFYING AS A RAFT OF BREAD
WITH BUBBLING CHEESE — AND THEY ALWAYS
BRING A LITTLE FLAIR AND EXCITEMENT.

# GARNISHES *and* ACCOMPANIMENTS

*S*ome sort of embellishment gives even the simplest soup a real lift and adds interest. Garnishes and accompaniments are especially important to complete and enhance the experience when soup is served as the main course.

*Soups embellishments can be anything from sauces to stir in, like Provençal basil purée with olive oil, to pasta parcels or herb dumplings, to a simple whirl of cream on top. The idea is to provide visual interest and a flavour lift.*

Bread in one form or another is the most common soup garnish. In fact, the earliest soup was hot liquid poured over bread and ever since, it has played an integral role in the consumption of soup. Croutons made from bread come in all shapes and sizes, breadcrumbs may be the binding for dumplings and bread itself is sometimes used as a thickener in puréed soups.

A simple loaf of crusty bread is often the most satisfying partner to soup.

## Other Embellishments

Some soups have traditional garnishes without which they seem incomplete. Fish soups in France are often served with garlicky mayonnaise-like sauces – *rouille* and *aïoli* – in addition to croutons. These can give a lift to other kinds of soup as well, such as Chicken Minestroni. These powerful sauces are best in robust soups, as is the basil purée from the Provençal Vegetable Soup.

Consommés and clear soups need embellishment and they offer a perfect opportunity to experiment with all sorts of garnishes. You can vary a soup significantly by changing its accompaniment. For example, you could put chicken quenelles in Tarragon Chicken Consommé, as in the recipe, or alternatively add herb dumplings, homemade noodles, poached quail eggs (all in this book) or other things you are likely to have handy, such as cooked rice, finely diced tomatoes or thin ribbons of spinach.

## Serving with Flair

It is difficult to give precise guidelines for anything as individual as creativity and style. The less confined you feel by rules, the better. Give your imagination free rein. Experiment and don't worry if it doesn't work out perfectly.

Create drama with colour contrast. This can be the whiteness of soured cream on deep red Borscht, a brilliant orange roasted pepper purée on pale brown aubergine soup or yellow nasturtium blossoms on asparagus soup. The Victorians had a penchant for creating a whole meal of food of the same colour, but dramatic impact is easier to achieve with contrast.

The attraction of most garnishes is the visual element, but a contrast of texture is also appealing. Crispy fried onions or crumbled bacon sprinkled over a creamy soup brings a delightful element of surprise.

Use something in an unexpected way, such as sprinkling thin ribbons of fresh spinach instead of chopped parsley when a herbal garnish is appropriate, or using whole sprigs of basil leaves instead of chopped ones. Something as simple as freezing mint leaves or other herbs or small pieces of fruit or vegetables into ice cubes destined to chill cold savoury soups or fruit soups makes a dramatic impression. What you freeze in these ice cubes should, of course, be clean and identifiable.

Select flavours that work together. For example, chive flowers would be better on Sweet Potato and Leek Soup than on Sesame Carrot and Parsnip because the chive flavour echoes the leek, both being of the onion family.

Edible flowers make simple yet appealing garnishes, as long as they have not been sprayed. Many supermarkets now carry edible flowers, so that is a good source. Avoid flowers from florists and nurseries, as these have usually been exposed to pesticides. The flowers of common culinary herbs are edible, so if you have a garden – or a friend who has – use basil, borage, chive, mint, rosemary and thyme flowers, among others. Equally, some fruit and vegetable blooms make a colourful garnish; try the flowers of beans, various squashes or cherries, again from a source you know. Not all flowers are safe to eat or use with food, so consult a specialist if you want to be sure. Otherwise stay with rose petals, primroses, pansies, violets, lavender, jasmine, geraniums, nasturtiums, hollyhocks and honeysuckle blossoms, preferably fresh from the garden and unsprayed.

~.~.~.~.~.~.~.~.~.~.~.~.~.~.~.~.~.~.~.~.~.~.~.~.~.~.~.~.~.~.~

# DECORATIVE ICE BOWL

Flowers, fruit and leaves glowing through ice formed into a bowl make a stunning presentation for a cold soup. You could use all herbs and herb flowers for a savoury cold soup or carry out the theme of a dessert soup by freezing the same fruit in ice. Make sure the ice bowl is large enough to hold what you plan to serve from it. You can make individual bowls if you have enough freezer space for them.

*Crushed Ice*
*2 freezer-safe bowls (preferably tempered glass),*
    *at least 2-l/3½-pt and 2.5-l/4½-pt capacities*
*Ice cubes or ceramic baking beans*
*A selection of two or three kinds of small edible*
    *flowers and other herb flowers and*
    *leaves, free of pesticides*
*A selection of two or three*
    *kinds of small fruit, such*
    *as blueberries,*
    *redcurrants,*
    *raspberries, small*
    *strawberries, cherries,*
    *grapes and halved kumquats*

**TO MAKE THE BOWL**
Put a layer of crushed ice in the bottom of the larger bowl. Set the smaller bowl inside and weight it down with ice cubes. Drop some flowers and/or flower petals, some leaves and some fruit into the space between the two bowls. Add some crushed ice to take up some space between the decorative elements and prevent them from floating. Continue filling the space between the bowls with flowers, fruit, leaves and crushed ice. Pour in cold water to come up to the rim of the larger bowl and freeze until firm.

To unmould, pour warm water into the smaller bowl and lift it out as soon as the ice around it starts to melt. Dip the larger bowl in warm water and turn the ice bowl out. If not using immediately, store it in the freezer.

For serving, set the ice bowl on a napkin on a tray or platter and decorate the base, if wished, with more leaves, flowers and fruit.

# Baked and Fried Garnishes

## CROUTONS

Croutons come in all shapes and sizes, depending on what they are served with, but their crunchy texture always adds interest. Most often, they are simply thin slices of baguette toasted until dry and crisp; these are almost invariably served with French fish soups. Croutons cut from larger diameter loaves, such as those used in classic French Onion Soup to support the cheese that is grilled on top, are sometimes called *croûtes*. They can also be made from brown or granary bread, brioche or other foods used like bread, such as polenta. Most croutons keep well and are easily made in advance, especially when you have stale French bread to hand.

**MAKES ABOUT 30, SERVING 6–8**

*30-cm • 12-in piece of French bread (baguette/French stick), about 5cm • 2in*   *diameter and weighing about 150g • 5oz*

❶ Preheat the oven to 180°C/350°F/Gas 4. Cut the bread into slices about 1cm/⅜in thick.
❷ Place the slices in one layer on a baking sheet and toast for 8–10 minutes, turning once, or until golden.
❸ Serve hot or allow to cool completely and store in an airtight container for up to 3 days or freeze, well wrapped. Serve at room temperature or warm before serving.

### Variations

If you wish, brush the croutons with olive oil after you turn them over. For garlic croutons, rub the toasts with a halved garlic clove after toasting. For a less intense garlic flavour, brush one side with garlic-infused oil after turning over. (To infuse the oil, combine finely chopped garlic with olive oil and set over low heat for about 10 minutes, or until aromatic.)

*CUBED CROUTONS* To make cubed croutons, cut crustless slices of firm sandwich bread or rustic country bread into 1.25-cm/½-in cubes. Place in a single layer in a Swiss roll tin and toast in a preheated 170°C/325°F/Gas 3 oven for about 20 minutes until golden, shaking the tin occasionally.
*FRIED CROUTONS* Both sliced and cubed croutons may be fried instead of toasted. Heat oil to a depth of about

1.25cm/½in in a small frying pan over medium-high heat. When it starts to smoke, add the croutons and fry until golden, stirring cubes or turning slices for even browning. Drain on paper towels and serve warm or at room temperature. (Best made within a few hours of serving; warm in a slow oven if made more than 15 minutes in advance.)

### Other Croutons

*POLENTA CROUTONS* Use polenta, moulded in a loaf tin until firm, then sliced thinly and cut in squares or diamonds. Cook as for Fried Croutons.
*SESAME CROUTONS* See Sesame Carrot and Parsnip Soup, page 38.
*GOAT'S CHEESE CROUTONS* See Roasted Tomato Soup with Goat's Cheese Croutons, page 38.
*CROSTINI* Crostini are essentially croutons with something on them. In Italy, the topping is often olive spread, anchovy paste, minced cooked chicken livers or cheese. A handy cheese spread for crostini is grated cheese, a little chopped onion and enough mayonnaise to hold it together spread on croutons and grilled.
*CORNMEAL FRITTERS* See Caramelized Onion Soup with Cornmeal Fritters, page 31.

## CHEESE STRAWS

These rich flaky pastries, although a bit fiddly, are worth the effort. They are perfect to accompany creamy vegetable soups, such as Emerald Soup or Cream of Asparagus Soup, as they provide a contrast of texture and taste. They are equally good served with drinks.

**MAKES ABOUT 50**

*200g • 7oz cold unsalted butter*
*200g • 7oz plain flour*
*135ml • 4½fl oz cold water*
*50g • 2oz freshly grated*
   *Gruyère or Parmesan cheese,*
*or a combination*
*1 egg, beaten with 1tsp water*
*3–4tbsp freshly grated*
   *Parmesan cheese*

❶ Cut the butter in 14 pieces and put into the freezer for 30 minutes, or until very firm.
❷ Put the flour into a food processor and pulse to combine. Add the butter and pulse three or four times; there should still be big chunks of butter. Run the machine for 5 seconds while pouring the water through the feed tube, then switch off the machine. Turn out the mixture on to a lightly floured cool work surface and gather into a flat ball. There should still be pieces of butter visible. If the butter is soft, chill the dough for 30 minutes or longer before proceeding.
❸ Roll out the dough into a long rectangle about 40 x 15cm/16 x 6in. Fold in thirds, bringing one side over to cover the middle, then the other on top of it, like folding a letter. Roll again into a long rectangle and fold again the same way (these are called "turns"). Chill the dough for 30 minutes.
❹ Roll out the dough into a long rectangle as before, sprinkle with about one-third of the cheese and fold in thirds. Repeat twice, sprinkling the dough each time with one-third of the cheese. Chill the dough, well wrapped, for at least 30 minutes or up to 3 days before using.
❺ Preheat the oven to 220°C/425°F/Gas 7. On a lightly floured cool work surface, roll out the dough to a thickness of 1cm/⅜in, brush lightly with egg and sprinkle with Parmesan. Using a long sharp knife, cut the dough into long thin sticks about 1cm/⅜in wide by 7.5cm/3in long. Place about 2.5cm/1in apart on large non-stick baking sheets and bake for 8–10 minutes until they are golden brown.

### *Variation*

If time is short, use 450g/1lb ready-made puff pastry and fold cheese into it as in the last two steps.

## PARMESAN PROFITEROLES

These little puffs are wonderful to garnish consommé or plain tomato soup. It is difficult to make a really small quantity of the dough, so enjoy the leftovers with a glass of wine – as they do in Burgundy.

**MAKES 50–60**

*65g • 2½oz plain flour*
*pinch of salt*
*pinch of freshly grated nutmeg*
*3 eggs*
*120ml • 4fl oz water*
*50g • 2oz unsalted butter,*
   *cut in 6 pieces*
*2tbsp freshly grated*
   *Parmesan cheese*

❶ Preheat the oven to 200°C/400°F/Gas 7. Lightly grease a large baking sheet.
❷ Sift together the flour, salt and nutmeg. Beat the eggs in a small bowl.
❸ Bring the water and butter to the boil in a small saucepan. When the butter has melted, remove from the heat and add the sifted dry ingredients all at once. Beat with a wooden spoon until well incorporated and the mixture starts to pull away from the sides of the pan.
❹ Set the pan over low heat and cook the mixture for 1 minute to dry it, stirring constantly.
❺ Off the heat, add about two-thirds of the beaten egg, beat thoroughly with a wooden spoon, then add a little more and beat to incorporate thoroughly. The dough should be smooth and shiny. Drop a little from the spoon; it should pull away and fall slowly. If it does not, add more beaten egg until the dough will drop slowly from the spoon. Stir in the cheese.
❻ Spoon the pastry into a piping bag fitted with a 1.25-cm/½-in plain tube and pipe the dough on the baking sheet in small mounds about 1.25cm/½in in diameter and about 4cm/1½in apart. Alternatively, using a small teaspoon, drop the dough in small mounds. Bake for 15–18 minutes until the puffs are well browned. Allow to cool in the turned-off oven with the door ajar.

# Other Garnishes

## SPICY GARLIC MAYONNAISE

### (*Rouille*)

This sauce, typically served with certain regional fish soups in France, takes its name from the rust colour that the pimiento, or roasted red pepper, gives it. Try it also to accompany cold turkey, chicken or shellfish, or to dress a pasta salad.

**MAKES ABOUT 175ML/6FL OZ**

*25g • 1oz soft white breadcrumbs*
*1–2 garlic cloves, very finely chopped*
*1 egg yolk, at room temperature*
*½ pimiento*
*1tsp tomato paste*
*175ml • 6fl oz extra-virgin olive oil*

❶ Soak the breadcrumbs in warm water and squeeze dry. Put in a food processor with the garlic, egg yolk, pimiento and tomato paste, and purée until smooth. With the machine running, slowly pour the oil through the feed tube, scraping down the sides as needed.
❷ Scrape into a serving dish or storage container. If not using immediately, cover and refrigerate for up to 2 days.

## Variations

*AIOLI*   See Garlic Fish Soup, page 84.
*BASIL PUREE*   See Provençal Vegetable Soup, page 22.

## CRISPY FRIED ONIONS

These crispy onions make an unusual garnish for creamy vegetable soups, but they are also good with sautéed or grilled poultry or meat. Several large shallots may be substituted for the onion.

**MAKES ABOUT 6 SERVINGS**

*1 large red or yellow onion*
*olive or ground nut oil, for frying*

❶ Cut the onion in half through the stem and remove the root end. Place cut-side down and slice very thinly. Blot the slices on paper towels.
❷ Heat oil to a depth of about 1.25cm/½in in a small deep frying pan over medium-high heat until it begins to smoke. Drop in about one-third of the onion slices and fry until deep golden brown. Using a slotted spoon, transfer to paper towels and drain. Cook the remaining onion slices in batches and drain. Sprinkle the onions lightly with salt, if you wish.

## DUMPLINGS

*CHICKEN QUENELLES*   See Tarragon Chicken Consommé with Chicken Quenelles, page 117.
*FISH QUENELLES*   Substitute 200g/7oz boneless white fish fillet for the chicken and parsley for the tarragon.
*HERB DUMPLINGS*   See Chicken Soup with Herb Dumplings, page 61.
*LIVER DUMPLINGS*   See Pheasant Soup with Liver Dumplings, page 65.

## PASTA

*RAVIOLI*   See Seafood Ravioli in Bouillon and variations, page 116.
*WONTONS*   See Wonton Soup, page 113. The filling may also be used for ravioli.
*NOODLES*   See Chicken Soup with Homemade Noodles, page 64.

# Index

# ACKNOWLEDGEMENTS

Pictor 6, 8–9, Stuart Frawley/Ace 11, Pictor 17, PictureBank 18–19, 21,
Mauritius/Ace 23, PictureBank 40–1, Fotopic/Ace 42, Trevor Wood/Image
Bank 57, PictureBank 68–9, 70, Zephyr Pictures/Ace 86–7, Allan Stone/Ace
88, Mauritius/Ace 89, Grant V. Faint/Image Bank 98–9, Pictor 100, 108–9, 111,
Alan Spence/Ace 118–9, Pictor 120, 122.
All other photographs are the copyright of Quarto Publishing plc.
Quarto would also like to thank Lee Pattison and Villeroy & Boch Tableware
Ltd, 267 Merton Road, London SW18 5JS; Oddbins UK Ltd, 31 Weir Road
Industrial Estate, London SW19 8UG and Agadir Restaurant, 84 Westbourne
Grove, London W2 for supplying props for photography.
Author's acknowledgements:
With my sincere thanks to Beverly Le Blanc and Philip Back for help with
recipe testing, Jessica Palmer for her invaluable input on many levels, and
most of all to my husband Tim Garland, for his patience with a steady diet of
soup, his thoughtful critical analysis and his fine palate.